Thinking about
almost everything

Thinking about almost everything

> new ideas to light up minds

Edited by Ash Amin and Michael O'Neill
with Donna-Marie Brown and Shari Daya

First published in Great Britain in 2009 by
PROFILE BOOKS LTD
3A Exmouth House
Pine Street
London ECIR OJH
www.profilebooks.com

10 9 8 7 6 5 4 3 2 1

All photographs by Andrew Heptinstall

The quotation from 'In Memory of W. B. Yeats' on page 27 is reprinted from *The English Auden* by permission of Faber and Faber Ltd.

A CIP catalogue record for this book is available from the British Library.

ISBN 978 1 84668 188 2

Text design by Sue Lamble
Typeset in Plantin by MacGuru Ltd
info@macguru.org.uk

Printed in Great Britain by
Clays Ltd, St Ives plc

Mixed Sources
Product group from well-managed forests and other controlled sources
www.fsc.org Cert no. TT-COC-002227
© 1996 Forest Stewardship Council
FSC

Contents

(Un)Settlement 87

Well-Being 115

Vision 133

Knowing

Rights

Futures

Preface

IDEAS ARE REMARKABLE things. They can transform our lives and have a huge impact on the world. They begin in someone's mind, triggered by a multitude of things, and as they grow and develop they are communicated to others. This process is fascinating – and contagious. The analogy between the transmitted idea (the Transmid) and an infectious agent is a useful one. It may be a potent idea, in which case it is rapidly transmitted and spreads quickly. On the other hand it may meet with resistance or even be destroyed. It can lie dormant or latent, only to be replicated again under favourable circumstances.

Which is why this book is so relevant and interesting. New ideas are occurring all the time in different areas of knowledge, many of which will not be familiar to us. Universities are the birthplace of these new ideas and it is fitting that this book should come from a university whose function is concerned with pushing back the frontiers of knowledge. Early on in this book's development three frontiers were identified, all of which are illustrated within its pages. The first is based on being right at the leading edge – the frontier of a particular subject. The second frontier brings different subjects together, at the interface of which different ideas meet and from which new ideas emerge. The third frontier relates to the public and their understanding and engagement with the new ideas and the public policies which flow from them.

New ideas are, of course, challenging, hence the relevance of 'resistance' in the Transmid model. However, universities, industry and commerce, public services and those who develop policy all need to keep abreast of the possibilities ahead. This book provides horizon-scanning across many disciplines, which may stimulate further discussion. If it does it will have achieved its purpose. Turn the page and see what's inside.

Sir Kenneth Calman

Acknowledgements

MANY PEOPLE HAVE helped in bringing this book to frui-tion. We are extremely grateful to our co-editors Shari Daya and Donna-Marie Brown for their ideas and hard work from start to finish. We also thank Matthew Scott, who was part of the editorial team before returning to New Zealand in 2007. It has been a pleasure to work with our contributors, who have responded with forbearance and thoughtfulness to editorial suggestions and interventions. Audrey Bowron managed the flow and completion of the typescript with great efficiency and cheerfulness, and we warmly thank her. Paul Forty at Profile Books has been an energetic, strict and creative editor, a rare and invaluable find these days. We owe a particu-lar debt to Michael Lavery for helping with the design and promotion of the book, and also for persuading Andrew Heptin-stall to take the captivating photographs that illustrate the themes covered in it. Finally, we wish to thank Sir Kenneth Calman, without whom this book would not exist. He con-ceived the idea of producing a book of this kind during his Vice-Chancellorship of Durham University, an idea fully sup-ported by Professor Christopher Higgins, the current Vice-Chancellor, who provides the postscript for the volume.

Introduction

Ash Amin and Michael O'Neill

Ideas, knowledge and universities

This book presents original thinking about a remarkable range of world-making phenomena, past and present. It is an experiment with the power and reach of the briefest possible summations of studied thought. Its aim is to reaffirm the value of ideas in an age besotted by the battle between truisms of fact and faith. It is also designed to provoke reflection on the ideas of value and their presentation. Many would argue that in our times of scientific and technological reasoning ideas help little in apprehending the ways of a plural and complex world. Such a world, it is thought, demands the insight of evidence measured against accepted theory, forensic observation, archaeological recovery, specialist knowledge, models that can grasp and anticipate complex phenomena. Can ideas – intimations of the possible or the probable – explain world-making phenomena such as the origins of the universe, the mechanics of vision, the structure of mass, well-being in an insecure world, how we think and feel?

Yes they can – as the essays tackling these very topics in the book reveal – by guiding thought in new directions. Ideas, in the shape of hypotheses, propositions, summations, disruptive questions, guide the process of discovery. They ensure that our research tools – now so prolific and sophisticated that we are inclined to leave our thinking to them – are used to produce genuinely new knowledge. Ideas are intrinsic to knowing and good ideas are essential for breakthrough discoveries. It seems strange to have to say this, but perhaps less so when we consider the exclusive emphasis placed today on evidence-based and policy-relevant knowledge by education and research bodies, politicians and practitioners, and a proliferating 'expert' industry that includes the media and consultancy. One effect of this over-indulgence in a particular form of knowledge is the downgrading of free thought and critical imagination.

This book shows how wrong such downgrading is. First and foremost, it reveals that the craft of formulating original and credible ideas involves considerable expertise, depth of knowledge, situated imagination, and constant interplay between thought and material, so that the new can be born out of the known. The essays are written by scientists, literary scholars, historians, musicologists, geographers, philosophers, archaeologists, anthropologists, and others, each using different traditions and tools of the trade – from laboratory instruments and clinical or archaeological observations to software, books and archives – and different methods of work – from experimental trials, data-gathering and computer simulations to participant observation, textual analysis and theoretical criticism. Many types of 'evidence', from the material to the symbolic, and from the mass data to the poetic line, are gathered and crystallised through thought, imagination, insight and curiosity, to formulate summations – ideas – that are far from idle speculation or judgements in the dark.

This pressure of distillation is what is common to the current volume's presentation of ideas as diverse as the existence of cosmic dark energy or extra space-time dimensions, the co-evolution of genes and culture, the entanglement of matter at a distance, the urban condition as the human condition, the Asianisation of the future, the idea of deriving benefit from housing without owning a single brick, uncertainty that cannot be eliminated from forecasting models, the power of elegy, poetry and the Web in coping with loss, or the significance of light for current and future awareness. The second section of this introduction dwells further on the ways in which some of these ideas coexist in the book.

The essays demonstrate the centrality of ideas in the process of reshaping interpretation of the known and illuminating the unknown. It is the idea – proposed, mulled over, tested, refined – that permits one to dare to claim, as the entries in this book do, that thinking, feeling, sensing and knowing are tangled together, that we were born to cooperate, that the archaeology of rubbish reveals the mysteries of climate change, that there might be extra space-time dimensions, that humanitarianism might feed war, that the arts can aid well-being, that how much we know is shaped by what we see, that software animates life and response to threat, that strong legacies link Europe and the East, as they do secularism and religion or rationality and irrationality. No ideas, no chance of the new.

And when expressed succinctly, as in this book, ideas provide a vantage point. They help get past the clutter and noise that makes up the everyday world, past the debris of history; they clear ground for new awareness. They do this in many ways: summarising a totality; tracing a legacy; seeing a hidden connection; uncovering an order; anticipating the future; projecting a model of being; seeing the big picture. They are also a tool for sensing life. As a 'sensing', at least in the way intended in this book, ideas must be placed close to the world, constantly tested by its complications, contingencies and changes, and intimately connected to its practices. The idea as sensing is not detached from the world, pretending privileged access to the hidden hand or universal totality. It is a summation, not a crystal ball, ready for verification, debate, disputation; a spark to thought, but still one with authority and insight. This is how the statements in the book on pornography, irrationality, music theology, inflammatory labelling, software, ordinary people, existential feelings, international law, theological secularism, biological regeneration, or immortality should be read.

Seeing ideas as a signpost, an invitation to thought, an intimation of possibility, a clearing in the ground, is not to ignore their power. Ideas make the world, for they are the guide to future practice. Even the flimsiest ideas rooted in prejudice and ignorance make history and form public culture. We know this from the number of times the precepts of science, belief or faith have become universal impositions in the hands of dogmatic leaders or through the circulations of fashion, public culture, and pedagogic formulae. Ideas, when mobilised, become the templates of thought and practice. The ideas in this book, too, come laden with such potential, forcing new belief, for example, in the power of art to improve health, science to extend life or sight, religion to temper extremism, feeling and irrationality to drive reason. This, however, is not the sole or main intention, though it is a welcome spin-off. Instead, the book is centrally concerned to invite critical and creative scrutiny of its offerings and their juxtaposition with similar ideas elsewhere in the text – a kind of republican intellectual citizenship – fully conscious, however, of the very real power of the idea, once settled, to make worlds.

Finally, a word on the setting behind the ideas offered in *Thinking about Almost Everything*. The ideas come from a university setting, and in the shape taken here, raise some important questions about the public role of universities. All the essays come from leading academics at Durham University, one of Britain's oldest and most prestigious seats of learning. Universities at their best are sites of discovery and proposition, engaged in uncovering things unknown, reinterpreting things known, explaining how things work and fit together, and clarifying what matters or should matter. They are – or should be – key sources of big and influential ideas. We use the word 'should' advisedly, because only too frequently this role has been compromised by pressure from stakeholders – from funding agencies and governments to opinion-makers and public commentators – to make university research serve known or short-term interests. Research must resolve immediate practical problems, it must nourish specialisation, it must enhance national competitiveness and social cohesion, it must be of policy relevance, it must follow tried and tested traditions. These are some of the familiar injunctions. The price paid is the loss of the time and freedom to think, risk, look beyond the boundary, make mistakes and, above all, cherish the desire to cultivate world-making thinking and practice.

Some universities, mercifully, manage to resist or get around these pressures, affording their scholars the space to develop big ideas, or at least ideas about the big ideas. Whether these ideas become known or influential is another matter. Again, only too frequently, they circulate in closed circles among specialists talking to each other, or when they are made public they come in narrow, indigestible, esoteric, trivialising or authoritarian form. They can come cloaked as instructions to thought, simplifications that lose meaning and bite, tomes that are difficult to grasp or sustain interest in, and complications of complexity. The purpose of this book is quite different; it is to communicate authoritative work on a spectrum of significant matters of being and knowing in a lively, open and accessible manner. The essays speak from and to serious work, but the aim is not to instruct, but rather to catalyse further thought and interest. In doing so, our hope is to show that universities can play a central role in shaping public opinion in a thinking society.

Thinking about Almost Everything: structure and mode

Writing in *To the Lighthouse* of 'illuminations, matches struck unexpectedly in the dark', Virginia Woolf might be describing what the editors of *Thinking about Almost Everything* feel the book gives its readers. The volume's structure is multi-faceted, honeycombed, intent on connections, contrasts, and interplay. Juxtaposition is its heart-beat and life-blood. Or, to revert to Woolf's metaphor, the matches struck unexpectedly in the dark will kindle, we trust, an intellectual bonfire. In assembling the book, we found ourselves delightedly overwhelmed by the variousness of and relationships between the offerings we received, and have sought, to adapt a phrase from the American poet Wallace Stevens, to discover an order, rather than impose one. Our nine headings – 'Legacies', 'Presences', 'Matter', '(Un) Settlement', 'Well-Being', 'Vision', 'Knowing', 'Rights' and 'Futures' – house a set of highly independent voices that share common or clashing inflections.

Each section might be thought of as a seminar series haunted and encouraged by the possibility of an enhanced collective knowledge. F. R. Leavis could be one of the more hectoring of literary critics when he didn't like a writer, but his adage that in reading literature 'minds meet' in the text is unsurpassed as an account of what happens or should be happening in teaching and reading. Leavis's idea also points us towards something close to an ideal of how a culture might function, one which microcosmically the current book embodies: that is, an intense conversation in which voices are raised, and even quibble or score points, but in which no one storms out of the room in a strop; rather, the participants (here the contributors and their readers) settle down to find a way forward, discovering radical disagreements perhaps, yet always staying alert to the value and power of differing views, searching, through thick and thin, to sustain communication, to understand the self and others, and, ultimately, to hold multiple thoughts in a single act of mind.

And not just the mind: Patricia Waugh's contribution to a section of interlocking essays on 'Knowing' recognises that 'thinking' and 'feeling' live one another's life; emotion has its reasons which reason both depends on and at times struggles to grasp. In the same section, Aidan Feeney and David Over explore the relationship between conditional reasoning and decision-making; Charles Fernyhough listens in to the far-reaching question of how voices 'get into the head'; Michael Goldstein addresses the question of how models relate to reality; Wolfram Hinzen advocates the notion of 'non-linguistic thought' if we are to acknowledge our kinship with the rest of the animal world; Boris Wiseman draws on Lévi-Strauss to renew our sense of how we think of, and with, the sensory world; Penny Wilson invites us to reconsider the supposed antithesis between scholarly drudgery and creativity; and Matthew Ratcliffe (recalling the emphasis of Waugh's piece) shows that feelings have taken on a new significance for philosophers. Emotion and feeling, grief itself, the subject of elegy, on which Stephen Regan writes eloquently in the section on 'Legacies', depend on our capacity to articulate, to find a language answerable to the depths of human need. Finding a language for a range of thoughts and feelings, *Thinking about Almost Everything* stages and stimulates a symphony of conversations.

Among the most significant of these conversations is that which the book sets in motion between scientists and the wider community. *Thinking about Almost Everything* includes a number of pieces that evoke the excitement and the importance of scientific thought, as examples from our section on 'Matter' reveal. Jon Davidson shows how the Earth's DNA is recorded in tiny archives: the crystals in a rock or the layers of a stalactite. Carlos Frenk addresses the question of cosmic dark energy, an energy that makes up most of the universe and causes its expansion to accelerate, but which, as yet, has found no plausible explanation in physics. Finding such an explanation, Frenk concludes, is at once possible and among the great challenges of this century's science. Elsewhere, Nigel Glover asks another deep and riddling question: where does mass come from? In his opinion, particle physicists are on the brink of a major breakthrough. And James Stirling adds a further bold brushstroke to the book's canvas of scientific thought when he points us in the direction of another major enigma, the question, that is, of the number of dimensions we live in: might there be more than four? Stirling shows how particle physicists are discovering that the scale of additional dimensions may be larger than has previously been thought. All these, and other contributions from scientists, show a restless spirit of inquiry and remind us of Blake's remark that what is now proved was once only imagined. Our book reveals that the imagination of scientists has an intensity comparable with that of creative artists. Elsewhere in the section on 'Matter' Ifan Hughes opens our eyes to the strange mysteries of 'quantum entanglement'; value is gleaned by John Chapman from the increasingly significant subject of 'rubbish' (Ray Hudson also confronts the issue of 'waste'); and Maurice Tucker ponders the insights made available by the geological record encoded in rocks.

We have alighted on our nine themes, working inductively, from the ground up. Each topic serves as a provisional but durable hub round which a set of contributions is able to spin, so many wheels carrying forward a larger vehicle whose final form must be given shape by the reader. A brief account of the seven sections not already adumbrated in any detail will illustrate how the book works. 'Legacies' opens with a piece by one of the editors, Michael O'Neill, on the ways in which past poems live again as new poems grow out of them. Other pieces in this section approach legacies from an archaeological or historical perspective: T. J. Wilkinson and Graham Philip brood over the speed and scale of destruction of archaeological sites, warning us that we won't be able to resurrect the past when the tell-tale shards and fragments remaining from it have been bulldozed out of existence. Underscoring the past's refusal to stay still is its capacity, if asked the right questions, to give new and surprising answers. Charlotte Roberts points out that DNA analysis of tuberculosis in ancient human remains can illuminate TB's origin and evolution, while Chris Scarre puts the menace of our current climatic problems into the perspective of huge passages of time. Whether this comforts or doesn't is, as Scarre concludes, uncertain; but to be offered a window onto such an unfamiliar way of thinking about the here and now is salutary. Other essays – Regan on elegy, Max Paddison on the avant-garde, and Paul Stephenson's advocacy of a Byzantine Europe – further the section's engagement with the ramifications of 'Legacies'.

Other sections also thrive on juxtaposition, on the ways in which ideas sweep in down the avenue of a particular discipline, only to meet up in a metropolis of the intellect. In 'Presences', a section concerned with the life of phenomena and their impact upon life, Ash Amin, the other editor of this book, unsettles our standard thinking about race by evoking practices of racial judgement that draw on a collective unconscious of racial codification. Amin suggests the near-unavoidability of such judgements and the terrifying danger their pervasiveness poses. In the midst of liberal-mindedness, we live in a welter of prejudice. The appeal to avoid the mischief of prejudicial judgement with which Amin's piece closes sits well with Tim Blackman's piece – the next in the book – in which he argues that the main evolutionary driver is not the 'selfish gene' but the 'cooperative gene'. Human beings, for selfish reasons, need to cooperate. Such pragmatic idealism has its own capacity to hearten, one of the many roles an idea can perform. It can also warn and admonish, as Amin's essay shows. Or it can delight, as the mind grapples with mathematical solutions accounting for the curvature of soap bubbles, the subject of the Willmore conjecture discussed by John Bolton. The case illustrates 'blue skies' thinking, pure thought that turns out to have many practical applications. 'Presences' is, too, a word with resonant theological meanings, and Bennett Zon and Carol Harrison propose the creation of a new interdisciplinary subject, 'Music Theology'. This subject will break out of the stranglehold exerted by semiotics, with its claim that all signs are constructed, and restore for us a sense of transcendence, of real presences reachable through art and belief. Remaining essays – on 'Genes versus culture' by Jamie Tehrani and Robert Layton, on 'Plant genetics for a sustainable agriculture' by Keith Lindsey, and on 'Humans and animals' by Christopher Rowe – confront us with the ongoing, present reality of debates to do with free will, the possibility of genetic transformation in plants, and Socratic and Platonic ideas of human nature.

Again, the result is to generate an ebb and flow of voices, which, set in dialogue with each other, constitute a tidal confluence. The section on '(Un)Settlement' indicates through its troubled bracketing how disturbed and complex human settlement has become, not least through the urbanisation which is the theme of Ash Amin's essay and, in 'lighter' mode, Joe Painter's. Painter pleads for us not to ask from our cities more than they can give; Jonathan Rigg comments on the increasing abolition of the division between rural and urban life; and Richard Reid writes about Africa's turbulent, identity-changing problems, and proposes local solutions to these problems, in accord, here, with Reuben Loffman, who champions a 'decentralised politics' for Africa. From different perspectives, T. J. Wilkinson and Mike Bentley discuss the ultimate challenge to human settlement: climate change. For his part, David Campbell looks at the relationship between images and humanitarianism while Stephen Graham advocates a precise use of a word that is the stuff of collective nightmares, 'terrorism'. At the same time, to be disturbed is also to experience a longing for serenity and content, and essays in the section on 'Well-Being' explore ways in which our enjoyment of life and sense of value might be enhanced: through engagement with Asian traditions of thought

(David E. Cooper); achieving health gains through social policy (Sarah Curtis); using the net to cope with grief (Douglas Davies); therapies involving ethically responsible experiments with stem cells (Chris J. Hutchison); an awareness of the role played by creativity in maintaining and restoring health (Jane Macnaughton); and the manipulation of viruses, so that the manifest enemy of health is co-opted into being its surprising ally (Paul Yeo).

Central to the book in every way is the concept of 'Vision', which gives its name to the next section of essays. Here, Colin Bain illuminates light's ability to assemble and shape matter on a microscopic scale, while John Findlay connects the process of looking to tacit knowledge. Giles Gasper reflects on light's all-pervasive metaphorical and conceptual significance in Western culture; David Parker argues that light-guided techniques are making and will make possible non-invasive methods that can give reliable information about health and disease; and Roy Quinlan is intrigued by the significance of the eye for past and future breakthroughs in medical research. In a more sombre twist to the section's theme, and illustrating the book's consciousness that ideas are protean and full of many-sided implications, Ray Sharples laments the pervasiveness of light pollution in modern society. In turn, Julian Wright wishes to refocus the sometimes skewed vision of historians by looking at the contribution made to history by ordinary people. In so doing, he sets up links with many of the debates about knowledge opened up in the book, debates that have at their heart a sense of the urgent need to look afresh, to start anew.

In our penultimate section on 'Rights', our contributors face with insight and optimism of the will (even if sometimes tinged by pessimism of the intellect) many of the most troubling concerns of our fractured, division-torn, post-Cold War age. Michael Bohlander urges, from a legal perspective, an altogether more respectful engagement with Shari'a law than is currently the case in the West; Christopher Insole invites us to turn secularism's apparatus of critique on itself, to open up a renewed and informed dialogue between religion and secular liberalism; Clare McGlynn and Erika Rackley address the question of extreme pornography, proposing a feminist introduction into debate and legislation of the notion (and reality) of 'harm'. One true idea that they seek to recover, and would build with care and circumspection into the legal process, is the belief that all people have worth and value. Like many of the book's contributors, Daniel Read pricks the bubble of a commonplace conception: that human beings are governed by rational choice. Not so, argues Read, in considering people's economic behaviour, an argument with direct relevance to the times in which we live. Alec Ryrie echoes the concern of other contributors with the impulse to herd human beings into pens of the mind, and proposes ways by which to hold at bay the evil of inflammatory labelling. Eleanor Spaventa concludes the section with a reminder that the fight against terrorism has led to an attack on traditional modes of democracy. She enters a forceful plea for a more binding formulation of the rights of personhood.

Our concluding section looks at 'Futures', a section in which essays take a chance even as they deal with hazard and probability. Or even the improbable, the possibility, discussed by Robert Song, with playful seriousness, of post-human immortality. Before that final throw of the intellectual dice, David Budgen speculates on the consequences of 'ubiquitous computing'; Anoush Ehteshami predicts a future dominated by Asia; Richard Gameson supplies a warning against the consequences of forsaking papyri and parchment for pixels; David J. Hunter imagines a National Health Service transformed from being a sickness service to one centred on health; and Susan J. Smith brings us back to the economic grounds of our being, offering a timely meditation on the risks of housing now and in the future.

This outlining of the contents and mode of our nine sections is meant to whet the reader's appetite for the remarkable provocations to thought and action offered by the book as a whole. *Thinking about Almost Everything* marries the written word to the visual eloquence of Andrew Heptinstall's arresting photographs. It gives modern form to a kind of thinking that thrives on the broken arc, not the fully rounded circle, which does not seek to exhaust a subject, but to stimulate further reflection. It's a kind of thinking that crosses times and cultures; wristy, risky, dancingly quick on its feet, it is alive in Nietzsche's aphorisms, in Zen koans, and (as a local energy) in Plato's dialogues. These essays work in such a tradition, a tradition of the fragment, the interrupted but continuing conversation, the glimpse that reaches beyond itself. All are so many stones thrown into the pool of the mind and feelings of the reader.

Poetic legacies

Michael O'Neill

THEMES OF TRADITION, imitation and originality run through poetry and writings about poetry since time immemorial, and are as old as Parnassus. But what is still under-investigated is how poetry composes a unique form of knowledge about poetry – and, since poetry condenses into itself central cultural preoccupations, a unique form of knowledge about culture. What is especially noteworthy is how the meanings of an older poem shift and change when read alongside a poem it has influenced. To read, say, Shelley's 'To a Skylark' after reading Ted Hughes's 'Skylarks' is to engage in a process of dialogue, awareness of difference, and reconfiguration. At the outset, one might wish to say that Shelley was interested in immaterial essences and Hughes in the toil and effort of physical existence; but Hughes's poem also alerts one to the fact that there is a strong sense of the physical in Shelley, too. In turn, Hughes's poem has more in common with Shelleyan idealism than at first seems to be the case. It is as though Shelley's words have been subtly altered by Hughes's, and Hughes's by Shelley's, as though each poem is a prism through which the other poem can and indeed must be seen in an altered light.

> the past will not lie still in its own imaginary museum

Literary critics are familiar with Harold Bloom's counter-intuitive ideas about poetic influence. In various works, starting with *The Anxiety of Influence*, Bloom proposed powerfully non-linear ways of re-imagining tradition. His idea of *apophrades*, or the return of the dead, among the most resilient of his famous six 'revisionary ratios', alludes, in one of its guises, to the sense that great poems give of antedating, having priority over, an earlier text. In such cases the later work makes us feel – Bloom argues – as though the earlier poem were imitating it: Milton can seem to have read too much Wordsworth, Keats too much Tennyson. No account of poetic influence can ignore Bloom's, or, indeed, avoid being influenced by it, and though we need not be in thrall to his sombre vision of poetry as a form of near-murderous, even patricidal imaginative strife, his ideas are a spur to new thought. In particular, one would wish to face down Bloom's own forceful pessimism and argue that influence is or can be a process by which the past is freed into creative relations with the present. The startlingly original response to Milton's *Paradise Lost* and Dante's *Commedia* by Romantic poets shows how the meanings of a poem may undergo transformation in the process of making possible hitherto undiscovered meanings for later writers. As Shelley puts it in *A Defence of Poetry*, in phrasing which resonates beyond literature and speaks more generally to the mobile dialogue involved in cultural transmission at its most fascinating, 'All high poetry is infinite; it is as the first acorn, which contained all oaks potentially.' The past will not lie still in its own imaginary museum; it resurfaces, surprising us as a later generation prompts it to re-awaken and take on a changed existence. New poems perform a double work of resurrection; they step out of the graves of old ones, which may, in turn, be reborn.

Bloom, H. (1973) *The Anxiety of Influence*. New York: Oxford University Press

Eliot, T. S. (1920) 'Tradition and the Individual Talent', in *The Sacred Wood*. London: Methuen

Newlyn, L. (1993) *'Paradise Lost' and the Romantic Reader*. Oxford: Clarendon Press

The death and life of the avant-garde

Max Paddison

NOTIONS OF 'ADVANCED MUSIC' and an avant-garde in the arts have played a prominent role in Western culture since the middle of the nineteenth century, particularly following the upheavals of the revolutionary years 1848–9 in Europe. Historians have argued that the resulting disillusionment led to a rupture between artists and their public, and a turning away from accessibility towards self-contained artistic experimentation. The sense of the artist as both exile and pioneer exploring new and untrodden territory endured well beyond the middle of the twentieth century.

The new accessibility that began to appear in the arts in the 1970s, which was particularly noticeable in music through the influence of minimalism and in general through the retreat across the arts to a new moderate mainstream, was welcomed by arts administrators and general public alike. This had the immediate effect that the ironies of Dadaism and Surrealism were easily commandeered for more entertaining purposes in the service of style and advertising, while the austerities and difficulties of high modernism were simply reclassified as outmoded and mildly absurd. The well-known TV lager before-and-after advertisement from the late 1980s neatly captures the prevailing spirit: lonely, alienated, angst-ridden artist/intellectual sits, head in hands, in his grubby garret, shot in expressionist black and white and with modernist, atonal, soundtrack music; he reaches for the can of lager

> modernism is clearly for nerds

and drinks desperately; instantly everything changes to full colour, outdoors with friends in a luscious landscape, with opulent romantic soundtrack music. Modernism is clearly for nerds.

Arguably the heroic age of the avant-garde is over, and the conditions that sustained it have disappeared. If this is so, then the implications for the survival of radical and innovative music today are not very encouraging. Nevertheless, in spite of the evident retreat from the position occupied by the experimental art of the 1950s and 1960s, and what many have seen as the subsequent capitulation to consumerism, elements of an avant-garde within Western art music appear to persist against all odds. Indeed, while retaining its autonomy, the new avant-garde has even transposed itself to the new conditions, absorbing diverse, but always cast-off and previously disregarded materials, and compelling us to look at them differently because of the changed structural context in which they are embedded. In contemporary art music, three otherwise very different composers who come to mind in this respect are Brian Ferney-hough, Helmut Lachenmann and Wolfgang Rihm. Their work presents new challenges to aesthetics and musicology.

Adorno, T. (1992) 'Vers une musique informelle' (1961), *Quasi una fantasia*, trans. Rodney Livingstone. London and New York: Verso

Jameson, F. (1991) *Postmodernism, or, The Cultural Logic of Late Capitalism*. London and New York: Verso

Williams, A. (1997) *New Music and the Claims of Modernity*. Aldershot: Ashgate

Elegy

Stephen Regan

ELEGY IS THE POETIC FORM and distillation of our common human response to loss. As an idea, it takes shape in the pastoral laments of Classical literature, with their strong emphasis on fertility rites, but it retains a powerful influence in contemporary civilisation, wherever there is a deeply felt need for consolation and renewal in the face of death. In the literary imagination, elegy functions as a counterpart to well-established rituals of mourning: it prompts the expression of grief and bewilderment; it idealises the deceased and preserves our memories of them among the living; and it offers consolation and reassurance, finding solace in the seasonal rhythms of nature or in sustaining moral, philosophical and religious ideals. Elegy is founded on paradox and contradiction. It needs to remember the dead, but it also needs to forget them; it holds in suspension the cruel certainty of loss and the assuaging possibility of resurrection. From Classical times to the present, elegiac poetry has functioned as a creative outlet for what Sigmund Freud in his seminal essay 'Mourning and Melancholia' (1917) termed 'the work of mourning'.

> elegy is founded on paradox and contradiction

The formal conventions of elegy include the ceremonial procession of mourners and the ritual laying of wreaths and floral tributes, the troubled questioning of deities and the anguished appeal to witnesses, the cathartic outbreak of anger, and the symbolic apprehension of light and water as emblems of renewal

and return. Some well-known elegies are essentially medita-
tions on lost values and opportunities, or on a lost way of life
(Thomas Gray's 'Elegy Written in a Country Churchyard' is a
notable example). However, most of the prominent elegies in
the English tradition are lamentations for an exemplary or
exceptional figure, often another poet: John Milton's 'Lycidas',
Percy Bysshe Shelley's 'Adonais', Matthew Arnold's 'Thyrsis',
Alfred Tennyson's 'In Memoriam', Algernon Charles Swin-
burne's 'Ave Atque Vale', Thomas Hardy's 'A Singer Asleep'.
Poetry itself is frequently a source of consolation, and poetic
immortality is proffered as a type of resurrection.

In modern poetry, especially since the First World War, the ide-
alising and consoling tendencies associated with elegy have
sometimes been regarded sceptically, if not brutally rejected.
The casual insouciance and de-idealising instinct in modern
elegy are memorably captured by W. H. Auden in his affection-
ate quip to Yeats: 'You were silly like us: your gift survived it all'
('In Memory of W. B. Yeats'). In Northern Ireland, in the midst
of prolonged political violence, the elegiac impulse has elicited
some of the most moving and haunting poems of the late twentieth century from such writers as Michael Longley and Seamus
Heaney. The past two decades have witnessed the spectacle of
national mourning on a massive, bewildering scale, reminding
us that the struggle to make sense of grief and loss is by no
means a private preoccupation. Nor is elegy the preserve of
published poets. A profound need for some shared sense of
consolation prompted hundreds of extravagant elegies for Prin-
cess Diana in August 1997, and left us with the unforgettable
image of hastily written notes of farewell, forlornly fluttering in
the choking New York air in September 2001.

Ramazani, J. (1994) *The Poetry of Mourning: The modern elegy from Hardy to Heaney.* Chicago and London: University of Chicago Press

Sacks, P. (1985) *The English Elegy: Studies in the genre from Spenser to Yeats.* Baltimore and London: Johns Hopkins University Press

Shaw, W. D. (1994) *Elegy and Paradox: Testing the conventions.* Baltimore and London: Johns Hopkins University Press

Health and welfare:
lessons from the past

Charlotte Roberts

WHAT LESSONS may be learnt from exploring the history of disease for a better understanding of health-care provision in an age when there are clear advances but also the return of old diseases?

Tuberculosis (TB), a bacterial infection, is a case in point. In 1988 TB was considered a conquered disease, and yet it is believed to be responsible for more illness and death today than any other bacterial pathogen (in both developed and developing worlds). In 2005 there were 8.8 million new cases, with 7.4 million in Asia/sub-Saharan Africa where 1.5 million people died. Total new cases continue to increase, mainly in Africa, the Eastern Mediterranean and Southeast Asia. Contributing factors include poverty, diets containing TB-contaminated foods, overcrowding, increased mobility through travel and migration, the presence of HIV, lack of access to health education and care, and multi-drug resistance.

TB was equally a problem in our ancestors' world. Bioarchaeological research has charted TB's first appearance in human remains from archaeological sites in Italy to around 6000 BC, with an increase through time seen with urbanisation, settled communities, animal domestication, and poverty. Key to understanding TB today, and why we have a problem with control, begins with the research on the genome of the organism that caused it, the genome being the set of heredity factors locked into the chromosomes inside the nucleus of the body cells. The research suggested that TB did not, as was once thought, affect humans through ingestion, but the human form of the disease was around first, having possibly been in the Old World for three million years. DNA analysis of TB in ancient human remains is also now shedding new light on TB's origin and evolution, showing the human rather than the animal form of the infection was most prominent; this supports modern DNA analysis.

Contemporary advances in research are helping us to see whether the strains of the tuberculosis organism are the same today. These advances could ultimately help clinicians better understand why TB remains a global problem, why there is drug resistance, and why particular strains are associated with specific geographic locations/populations.

Roberts, C. A., Buikstra, J. E. (2008) *The Bioarchaeology of Tuberculosis: A global perspective on a re-emerging disease.* Gainesville, FL: Florida University Press

World Health Organization (2007) *Global Tuberculosis Control.* Geneva, Switzerland: World Health Organization

Zink, A. R., Sola, C., Reischel, U., Grabner, W., Rastogi, N., Wolf, H., Nerlich, A. G. (2004) 'Molecular identification and characterisation of *Mycobacterium tuberculosis* complex in ancient Egyptian mummies', *Int. J. Osteoarchaeology* 14: 404–13

Humans and climate: the long-term perspective

Chris Scarre

WE LIVE IN AN AGE of growing environmental uncertainty. Hardly a week passes without us hearing that we have had the wettest month for fifty years or the hottest summer since records began. For archaeologists (especially prehistoric archaeologists), accustomed to working on timescales of thousands or tens of thousands of years, however, current climate concerns take on a rather different (if still somewhat menacing) hue.

On the one hand, awareness of the *longue durée* emphasises that humans are both a tropical species and a product of the ice ages. We are tropical in our physiology and in our closest living relatives, the African apes; and one of the key themes within archaeology is the development of technologies – clothing, tools and fire – that enabled human ancestors to cope with temperate and cold environments. The successive advance and retreat of the ice sheets in the northern hemisphere have been recognised for more than a century, but evidence from

> humans are both a tropical species and a product of the ice ages

the Greenland ice cores (notably the GRIP core) has revealed that ice age climates were not merely cold, dry and generally hostile but were also characterised by high-amplitude variations that changed climate dramatically in periods ranging in length from a millennium to as little as a few decades. The past 10,000 years, by contrast, have been not only warmer than the previous glacial phase but also considerably more stable.

In the warmer, wetter postglacial world, populations grew rapidly. Even before the last cold phase had ended, intensive patterns of plant use had been developed that were the precursors to agriculture, and allowed populations to grow still further. New domesticates were developed to cope with colder climates and shorter growing seasons, in a forerunner to modern initiatives with GM crops, and new forms of social structure were established to cope with larger and increasingly agglomerated populations.

Yet growing human numbers have also inexorably and fundamentally altered that world, through steadily increasing emissions of methane and CO_2 that some believe may have averted the natural cyclical return to a new ice age. That is an unforeseen and unintended consequence, but as we move into an increasingly insecure environmental future, the study of the past highlights a troubling paradox. Humans owe their success not to a tight physiological adaptation to particular environments but to cultural adaptation – to being smart, flexible and inventive. The remarkable discovery that human populations in Europe grew strongly in one of the coldest phases of the last ice age underlines that it is through skill that humans grapple with adversity. Yet the human past is also punctuated by patterns of spectacular but unsustainable growth. The decline or collapse of early historic Maya and Moche societies illustrate the outcomes that may ensue when resources are no longer secure, while the deforestation of Easter Island warns us that human prescience has its own limitations. Should climate in the future revert to its more usual Pleistocene pattern of short-term large-amplitude fluctuations, we are in for a bumpy ride.

Burroughs, W. J. (2005) *Climate Change in Prehistory: The end of the reign of chaos*. Cambridge: Cambridge University Press

Peterson, L. C., and Haug, G. H. (2005) 'Climate and the collapse of Maya civilization', *American Scientist* 93: 322–29

Ruddiman, W. F. (2005) *Plows, Plagues and Petroleum: How humans took control of climate*. Princeton: Princeton University Press

A Byzantine Europe

Paul Stephenson

THE EUROPEAN UNION has set out in search of its common history, commissioning international research projects and funding exhibitions and conferences. Where should it look? The Roman Empire, which stretched across Germania and Gaul, incorporating the barbaric island of Thule (Britannia), will not do. First, since the Enlightenment, Rome has served as a model for numerous oppressive regimes. Rome was aggressively militaristic and politically conservative: hardly the template for an incipient twenty-first-century superpower. Second,

Rome's was a Mediterranean empire, geographically marginal to the core of the EU, containing regions the new Europe feels better without. With Carthage under excavation, we do not need St Augustine of Hippo to remind us that Rome reached to North Africa. Indeed, many in Germany and France do not want to be further reminded of Europe's links with those regions, as they experience problems associated with post-colonial immigration. Beyond Istanbul, the magnificent ruins at Ephesus in Turkey bear witness to that country's 'Roman-ness'.

> Byzantium has been left on the sidelines

Not Rome, but Latin Christendom has until now been chosen by the EU as an acceptable precursor. Forged from the 'barbarian' successor states of Rome, it emerged in the Middle Ages with its core in northern Europe. The single figure most greatly revered was Charlemagne, a ruler of both Germans and Franks, crowned emperor in Rome. A recent, massive European Science

Foundation research project, 'The Transformation of the Roman World', supported conferences and exhibitions across the EU. Tens of thousands attended five major exhibitions, including 'Heirs of Rome' at the British Museum. Byzantium, which endured even as the 'barbarians' carved out successor states from the western rump of the empire, has been left on the sidelines. Where does this leave the countries of eastern and southeastern Europe, and beyond, for which Latin Christendom is not the past? Should the eastern empire not also serve as a model for Europe, notably in its interactions with the Middle East?

Until the admission of Cyprus in May 2004, the only Byzantine heir within the EU was Greece. But with the accessions of Bulgaria and Romania in January 2007, the number of Byzantine heirs is now four, with several more hoping for future admission, including Albania, Croatia, Serbia, the Republic of Macedonia, and Turkey. Byzantium has left a deep imprint on all these national cultures, and with it many residual tensions. Romania and Bulgaria have resorted to medieval history and archaeology to demonstrate prior claims to the rich agricultural lands of the Dobrudja. Before and since Yugoslavia, southern Slavs have struggled to assert or deny their Byzantine heritage, and this has frequently taken the form of the destruction of medieval monuments. Albanians claim descent from a proto-European people, the Illyrians. But the Albanian lands were a crucial part of the Byzantine world, where natives of eastern and western Europe met to trade, as the recent excavations at Butrinto magnificently demonstrate. It is imperative that the diversities and commonalities of these post-Byzantine states are more fully explored and integrated within a broader European framework, just as the diversities and commonalities of Latin Christendom were explored in the 1990s.

Magdalino, P. and Ricks, D. (eds.) (1998) *Byzantium and the Modern Greek Identity*. Aldershot: Ashgate

Obolensky, D. (1971) The *Byzantine Commonwealth. Eastern Europe 500–1453*. London: Weidenfeld and Nicolson

Culture expunged

T. J. Wilkinson and Graham Philip

THE PRESENT GENERATION of archaeology students could be described as the 'Last Generation' because future researchers are unlikely to witness archaeological sites and landscapes as coherent remains. Such is the speed and scale of destruction that entire landscapes, archaeological sites and their contents are disappearing. Looting and pillaging are not the only culprits. Settlement sprawl, bulldozing of land for agriculture, and seemingly beneficial activities, such as the drainage of wetlands or irrigation schemes, are also implicated. A century ago (and far more recently in some areas), it was possible to see entire landscapes dominated by archaeological sites. A case in point is the vista of ancient mounds that Layard witnessed when he looked out from the citadel of Tell Afar in the nineteenth century (now within northern Iraq). Although such landscapes do remain, they are threatened on every side.

> the sheer complexity of the process of loss is remarkable

This loss can be categorised into three sections: a) archaeological *landscapes* that contain archaeological sites; b) the *sites*, their buildings and rubbish dumps (which often contain most information); and c) the *contained artefacts* (often the objects of looting). Just as archaeologists have developed sophisticated ways to retrieve evidence from progressively more difficult contexts, these resources are being destroyed. The sheer complexity of the process of loss is remarkable. Wars, or the loss of state power for other reasons, result in a breakdown of authority.

This encourages looting, which feeds the global antiquities trade, enriching wealthy collectors and some museums. Conversely, peace encourages agricultural, urban and infrastructural developments which can obliterate sites and entire landscapes. If unmanaged, the future looks gloomy in either direction.

While damage to present-day infrastructure is deplorable, with finance and skills it can be rebuilt. Archaeological remains once destroyed cannot be replaced. This catastrophic loss of cultural resources is one that the global community must deal with urgently. Future generations, if deprived of the means to investigate their heritage, will not easily understand our inaction. While there is already legislation in place from UNESCO, Interpol and other public authorities, more is required to prevent this loss. There are ways in which we can recognise, describe, communicate and perhaps safeguard such remains. For example, recent advances in technology, especially satellite remote sensing, enable us to monitor this destruction. Time-series images, spanning the late 1960s to the present day, demonstrate the scale and speed of destruction of the archaeological landscape and identify where protective measures are most urgently required. In terms of global warming, sophisticated modelling of sea-level change combined with more reliable archaeological inventories allows the identification of areas at high risk of significant damage, and upon which efforts can be focused.

Although these various agents of destruction have long been known and documented, the complexities of the threat are legion: economic development, population pressure, local conflict, ideological differences (leading to destruction of monuments), and environmental change all contribute to this loss. The cessation of development is unrealistic, and growing pressure on world resources means that any feasible solution will involve compromises. International agencies must encourage governments to take heritage protection as seriously as the development of prime sites for tourism. At a local level, communities should be encouraged to value and engage with heritages from which many feel distanced. If this task is not taken forward immediately, it will be too late.

Brodie, N., Doole, J. and Renfrew, C. (eds.) (2001) *Trade in Illicit Antiquities: The destruction of the world's archaeological heritage.* Cambridge: McDonald Institute for Archaeological Research

Fowler, P. (2004) *Landscapes for the World: Conserving global heritage.* Bollington, Cheshire: Windgather Press

Rahtz, P. (1974) *Rescue Archaeology.* Harmondsworth: Pelican

legacies

presences >

matter

(un)settlement

well-being

vision

knowing

rights

futures

endmatter

The racialisation of everything

Ash Amin

RACE THINKING has always relied on fictions of biological or cultural incompatibility to justify the categorisation and condemnation of others judged as dangerous or inferior. But these fictions change, and how they do so is of great significance in sustaining or combating practices of race in a given historical moment. The claim here is that a new language of race is emerging, melding with an older tradition of judgement, rooted first in biology and later in culture. This new language thrives on quick-fire judgements of surface bodily

> racism works through deep-rooted legacies

features, read as proxies of race. It signals a new kind of racism – a 'phenotypical' racism, freed from the definitional rigours of its antecedents, and therefore able to condemn human difference in dangerously promiscuous ways.

First, a short history of the idea of race. Darwin insisted on the unity of the human race, on seeing the peoples of the world as members of one family. But this did not prevent a detailed science of racial classification from emerging shortly after his time, a 'science' of eugenics that tore into the idea of unity. It set about separating humans into races on the basis of their biological and physical attributes, and then projected civilisational worth onto these differences, warning also of the dangers of mixture or maintenance of 'weaker stocks' for the evolutionary process. The result of such thinking is the all-too-familiar history of biological racism justified on grounds of nature's orders, manifest in its most extreme forms during Nazism and

Apartheid, and more recently in the tragedies of Bosnia and Rwanda. Biological racism has not disappeared – and indeed may even reappear through misuses of new genomic science involving arguments that the genetic make-up of certain ethnic and racial groups makes them more vulnerable to particular pathologies of ill-health, criminality or social apathy. However, its mooring in a sure science of racial difference and incommensurability has become unsteady, partly as a result of the rise of a more exact science revealing that over 90 per cent of genes are shared by all humans, with the remaining 10 per cent showing no significant variation between so-called races.

One response to growing world awareness of the barbarism of biological racism and to the insights of new genetic science has been the rise of new arguments justifying racial incompatibility. One of the results is cultural racism. 'We/they should be left free to practise our/their own customs and live with our/their own people' is its rallying cry, invoked as much by majorities justifying the exclusion of racialised others, as by minorities fighting for rights or spaces of their own. Culture, or, more accurately, the assumption that ethnic and racial groups possess fixed and distinctive cultural identities which they hold most dear, has become the excuse and explanation for separation, treading a thin line between celebrating and condemning difference. Cultural racism has no sympathy with the view that in a globalising world, identities are becoming mixed, plural and fast-changing. This certitude, which reduces complex processes of human engagement to matters of group culture, permits easy projection of the collective concerns of a society onto a photo-fit image of the Other. Once the connection between group identity and collective well-being has been made, all manner of racialised judgement is made possible. Accordingly, when, for example, a collective senses a threat to its stability and security, cultural racism permits the threat to be named with speed and clarity (as revealed by the coincidence today in the West between obsessive interest in Islam and Muslims and anxieties over terrorism and the religious state). This explains the quick shift we are witnessing in many western societies today from a mood of celebration of ethnic and cultural pluralism and mixture to a mood of suspicion and discipline towards the 'stranger', intent on personifying the habits and mores that offend, so that the wayward can be domesticated or crushed.

Many commentators on race argue that the history of racism is one of older forms giving way to newer ones. The thesis proposed here is that the history is one of accretion and endurance, of past latency that keeps race thinking always close to the surface, ready to spring into action when triggered, ever menacing. Thus, for example, the legacies of biological and cultural racism ensure that diverse modes of sensing human difference become interpreted as racial codes. Our senses constantly process phenomenological information based on what we see, smell, hear or touch into intellectual and emotional response, based on rapid assimilation and categorisation, with most of this work done pre-cognitively, tacitly, intuitively, even neurologically. It could be argued that one powerful subconscious ordering mechanism is a reflex of race, shaped by legacies of prehension, acting like cultural genes transmitted subliminally between generations. Only a mechanism of this sort can explain the instantaneity and endurance of racialised interpretation of the 'stranger', stimulated by the flicker of an eyelid, a bodily attribute, the sweep of a gesture, the trace of an utterance. Such a possibility is intimated in Arun Saldanha's book *Psychedelic White*, which reveals how the play and reception of 'Whiteness' and White superiority on the beach in Goa relies on bodily summaries of travel experience, skin colour, posture and gait, dress code and markings, accent, drawl and consumption habits, and presence on the beach at certain times and in certain spaces.

Reliance on bodily interpretation as a proxy for race has become commonplace, aided by the latency of master racial narratives. And as such, it dispenses with any need for a compelling science of race in the way that biological racism required, and is also freed from the limits of cultural racism, since any marker of difference that sticks to the body of the stranger with a measure of consistency will suffice. Phenotypical racism – based on reflexive response to surface phenomena – is flexible and mobile, allowing more and more telltale signs to be added, without much need for explanation or accuracy. The beard, the skull-cap, the ruck-sack, the hennaed hair, the baggy trousers: each is enough to signal the racial other even if none of the markings has anything to do with race. On most occasions, these evaluations generate watchfulness towards the now racial-ised stranger. But in times of charged public anxiety towards the stranger such as the present – with world affairs interpreted as a war of civilisations and cultures – the evaluations come charged with devastating mischief. On these occasions, the racialisation of everything threatens to encamp and destroy minorities, strangers, asylum seekers, races invented by the day; bearing the full force of phenotypical, biological, and cultural racism.

Fanon, F. (1967) *Black Skins, White Masks.* New York: Grove Press

Gilroy, P. (2004) *After Empire.* London: Routledge

Parekh, B. (2008) *A New Politics of Identity.* Basingstoke: Palgrave

Born to cooperate

Tim Blackman

ALTHOUGH SOCIOBIOLOGY is discredited among most social scientists these days, the Darwinian idea that there are processes of social and cultural evolution at work is still influential. The big idea that social science has introduced into this thinking, however, is that the evolutionary driver is not the 'selfish gene' but the 'cooperative gene'. An even bigger idea is that the outcome of these cooperative processes is a phenomenon worthy of study in its own right: complexity. From the earliest biochemical interactions at the start of life on earth to present-day global flows of money, ideas and people, evolution has driven growing complexity.

Cooperation, paradoxically, is a selfish strategy. Cells, animals, communities and societies tend towards cooperative behaviours because they achieve benefit for all; win-win interactions that evolutionary processes select for and exploit. There are exceptions, not least extinctions and wars. But in the long run it is the win-wins that drive change, with one very important consequence. These strategies have built higher and higher

> the evolutionary driver is not the 'selfish gene' but the 'cooperative gene'

levels of complexity in the natural world, and, since the emergence of humans, have also done so in the economic and social worlds.

Many conflicts arise from perceptions among the conflicting parties that outcomes are zero sum. One side has to win or else it will lose. Yet over time what is apparent is that non-zero sum solutions tend to emerge. This often happens by moving up a level in how a problem is understood and tackled, with an associated growth in complexity. Take the example of ageing societies like the UK. There is considerable potential for conflict between generations as a shrinking pool of workers face the bill for the pensions and care costs of a growing number of older people. There is no solution to this if it is regarded as a zero-sum problem. But if science and technology enable work to become more productive and ageing to be less disabling, all are winners because the economy can support more older people and their cost to public services is contained.

This does not just happen. There is a need for macroscopic vision: ways of seeing and acting on the big picture. There is a vital, democratic role here for the social sciences. We can, thanks to good data and demographic methods, see our emerging ageing society. We can then, as a society, do something about it.

Byrne, D. (1998) *Complexity Theory and the Social Sciences.* London: Routledge

Chapman, J. (2004) *System Failure,* 2nd ed. London: Demos

Wright, R. (2000) *Nonzero: History, Evolution & Human Cooperation.* London: Abacus

Soap bubbles:
the Willmore conjecture

John Bolton

ALTHOUGH NATURE often seems profligate, much is governed by the drive for efficiency and the desire to minimise effort. For instance, if you dip a wire frame into a soap solution and pull it out so that the frame is spanned by a soap film, the beautiful and artistic shape that results is the surface of minimal area bounded by the wire. Not only is this efficient, it is usually very strong, which is why several, rather spectacular, roofs are based on the shape of a soap film. Soap film surfaces are very interesting mathematically, and may be investigated using a branch of mathematics, differential geometry, which concerns itself with curvature. The average curvature at each point of a soap film surface is zero; the surface is saddle-shaped at each point, and the upward and downward curvatures are equal and opposite. The surface of a football, or a soap bubble, doesn't have this property, since at each point the curvature is the same in all directions. Soap bubbles minimise the area of a surface enclosing a given volume (of air), while soap films minimise the area spanning a wire frame. A soap bubble is a surface with finite area and no boundary, but every finite-area soap-film surface must have a boundary (formed by a supporting wire frame). By calculating over the surface the (square of the) average curvature at each point, we obtain a measure of how far the surface is from being a soap-film surface. By this measure, the surface of a football is nearer to being a soap-film surface than, say, the

> a soap bubble is a surface with finite area and no boundary

surface of a rugby ball. In fact, no matter how you deform the surface of a football, you cannot decrease this total amount of average curvature.

We now consider the same problem for the next-simplest family of surfaces with finite area and no boundary, namely those surfaces which are deformations of the surface of a doughnut. These surfaces have one hole (while a pretzel, for instance, has three).

The question is: which such surface is closest to being a soap-film surface, in the sense that it has the smallest possible total of the square of the average curvature, and what is this smallest total? This seemingly innocuous question was first asked in the mid-1960s by Professor T. J. Willmore of the Department of Mathematical Sciences at Durham University. He also suggested the answer, now called the Willmore conjecture, that this smallest total was equal to twice the square of pi (where, as usual, pi denotes the ratio of the circumference of a circle to its diameter). Since then, many high-powered mathematicians world-wide have tried to decide whether Professor Willmore's guess was correct. This has inspired the development of a rich vein of mathematics, and a whole new class of surfaces, called Willmore surfaces. It has also aroused strong passions and much controversy; several mathematicians have claimed a proof of the Willmore conjecture, but their proofs have either been incorrect or have been so convoluted that other mathematicians have not been able to check them. The jury is still out.

This may seem like the purest of pure mathematics, but, as is the case for other branches of pure mathematics, Willmore surfaces now have important practical applications: they are much used in computer-aided design and in the study of cell membranes. If you would like to know more, or see some beautiful pictures of Willmore surfaces, then type 'Willmore surface' into an internet search engine.

Leschke, K. and Pedit, F. (2008) 'Sequences of Willmore surfaces', *Mathematische Zeitschrift* 259: 113–22

Willmore, T. J. (1971) 'Mean curvature of Riemannian immersions', *J. London Math. Soc.* (2) 3: 307–10

Willmore, T. J. (1993) *Riemannian Geometry*. Oxford and New York: Oxford University Press

The interdiscipline of music theology

Bennett Zon and Carol Harrison

MUSIC AND THEOLOGY remain largely separate disciplines, despite sharing a long and frequently interrelated history. Today, however, recent scholarship has begun to erode disciplinary barriers, fostering a rich, genuinely interdisciplinary discourse. It is our aim to investigate this discourse, and from these investigations to identify and develop an 'interdiscipline' called Music Theology.

This dynamic unity, which is often inherent in classical and medieval works, such as Augustine's *De Musica* or Boethius's *De Institutione Musica*, has been attenuated as both Music and Theology, from the late middle ages, adopted and evolved increasingly scientific models of specialisation, often distinguished by theoretical and practical divisions in methodological praxis. Jeremy Begbie, in *Theology, Music and Time*, has called these divisions 'unnecessary polarisations', and speaks within the interdiscipline of Music Theology when he postulates 'music's interconnectedness' with theology as its *modus vivendi*. An example of this is Andrew Love's observation, in *Musical Improvisation*, that the nature of musical improvisation provides a universal locus for Christian hope.

> music is 'beyond art, a real presence that we venerate'

Unlike other disciplines, Music Theology responds to an audience increasingly sceptical of critical thinking which presupposes the cultural construction of signs, and offers an alternative theoretical framework in which notions of mystery, transcendence and sacramentality can inform critical investigation. Where Daniel Chua, in *Absolute Music and the Construction of Meaning*, can look to high Renaissance musicology as a point in which music's 'supernatural aura [was] demystified as natural and its inaudible, invisible essences dismissed as non-existent', Music Theology restores and interrogates the applicability of earlier holistic frameworks. These frameworks are especially relevant today, as composers, performers, listeners and writers seek ways of musical and theological interpretation. Thus, from a musical standpoint, John Tavener suggests that music is iconic, 'beyond art, a real presence that we venerate'.

Given the highly diversified nature of ideologies within theology and musicology, Music Theology must, and will, by necessity engage inclusively with the full spectrum of intellectual paradigms informing our current cultural horizon – from patristics to post-modernism.

Begbie, J. (2000) *Theology, Music and Time*. Cambridge: Cambridge University Press

Love, A. (2003) *Musical Improvisation, Heidegger, and the Liturgy*. Lewiston, NY: Edwin Mellen Press

Genes versus culture

Jamie Tehrani and Robert Layton

IS THERE TRULY such a thing as conscious choice or 'free will'? Or are we kept on a tight leash by the powerful instincts handed down to us by our prehistoric ancestors? Richard Dawkins famously described the individual as little more than a 'survival machine', programmed and controlled by genes that have their own 'selfish' agenda. Usually, what is good for the gene is good for the individual, because our genes need us to survive and reproduce so that they are passed on – which is why they have designed us to enjoy food and sex. The problem is that there are also occasions when the interests of the gene may conflict with those of the individual. Think of the worker-bee who is prepared to sacrifice his own life in order to protect his colony. From the gene's point of view, what matters is not the survival of the individual, but the survival of the queen bee who produces the eggs from which future carriers of the gene will hatch.

Of course, human beings are not the same as honey bees. People are not driven to commit acts of martyrdom or suicide by their genes but by their own personal choice, however perverse. Many social scientists believe that humanity is no longer subject to biological natural selection at all. This is because culture allows us to acquire behaviours and attitudes from many people, not just our parents, giving us a greater capacity to shape our own lives. Evolutionary psychologists, on the other hand, argue that it is misleading to treat the mind as an empty vessel, to be filled with learned social rules. Instead, they propose that, even in modern industrial contexts, we continue to think in ways that were originally designed to cope with the adaptive challenges faced by our hunter-gatherer ancestors, such as who to mate with, when to cooperate with others, and how much parental care to expend on each offspring.

In recent years, there has been an effort to map out a middle path between these two contrasting visions. The new paradigm of 'cultural evolution' explores the ways in which our behaviour is influenced by the complex and sometimes antagonistic interactions between biology and culture. For example, cultural transmission among members of a tribe of hunter-gatherers can speed up the rate at which more efficient foraging strategies are adopted. It follows that those who are most attuned to observing and learning from others are likely to have greater reproductive success than those who are less so. This leads us into the delicious paradox that is at the heart of cultural evolutionary theory. For, while a predisposition to imitate others is central to the adaptive success of humans, it also leaves us susceptible to the adoption of traits that are of no use to our survival, or which may even be dangerously maladaptive.

> what is good for the gene is good for the individual

Let us consider again the case of suicide. Sociologists since Durkheim have known that the incidence of suicide in a population tends to follow a predictable pattern, whether it is in Scandinavia or the South Seas, and regardless of the innumerable personal reasons that lead to individuals making such tragic choices. We are now beginning to develop models to capture the dynamics of such cultural epidemics by focusing on who copies what from whom, and under what regimes of influence. These models promise to provide insights that will be applicable in fields as diverse as marketing, education, development and electioneering. But the widespread and successful transmission of behaviours harmful to individuals such as

suicide, drug-addiction and anorexia raises a disturbing possibility: what if we are being programmed by not just one class
of selfish replicators, but by two? What if culture is not the lib-
erator of individual free will, but another jailer?

Dawkins, R. (1976) *The Selfish Gene*. Oxford: Oxford University
Press

Laland, K. and Brown, G. (2002) *Sense and Nonesense – Evolutionary
perspectives on human behaviour*. Oxford: Oxford University Press

Richerson, P. and Boyd, R. (2005) *Not by Genes Alone – How culture
transformed human evolution*. Chicago: University of Chicago Press

Plant genetics for a sustainable agriculture

Keith Lindsey

THE YEAR 2009 marks the 200th anniversary of Charles Darwin's birth. It is also 150 years since he published his seminal work, *On the Origin of Species*. Since then, the industrial revolution has transformed our lives, for good and bad. Atmospheric CO_2 levels have increased. Fossil fuel reserves are declining, threatening energy security. The human population, 1.2 billion in 1850, is currently 6.6 billion and is set to increase to over 9 billion by 2050; it needs to be fed in the face of a declining availability of arable land. Darwin's work spawned a revolution in agriculture, through the recognition that species are not fixed, but evolve. Mendel's work on peas a few years later in turn sowed the seeds of our understanding of the genetic basis of evolution, and indeed of life itself.

How can genetics help solve these problems facing mankind? Plants are central to the solution. They absorb CO_2, produce oxygen, and are the source of staples critical for human survival. They are also essential for non-food uses, including pharmaceuticals and forestry. Increasingly important will be the use of plants in sustainable energy production, as a source of starch, oils and cellulose as raw materials for biofuels.

The biology of plant exploitation is complex and fascinating, and raises many fundamental questions. Why do some species produce valuable products, while others do not? Why do species look different, and indeed, how different are they? These are questions of identity. If we can understand this, what are the implications for the economic exploitation of plants, for food and non-food uses?

The critical genetic differences between plant species may be relatively small. Although the cress plant *Arabidopsis thaliana*, for example, has a genome of about thirty thousand genes (slightly more than humans), recent research suggests that major differences between plants may be controlled by only a very small fraction of these genes. The key classification characters of plants, differences in the structures of flowers and leaves, may present a falsely exaggerated picture of the evolutionary differences.

There is an increasing body of evidence to support this view. For example, mutation of single genes can convert asymmetric flowers (as seen in orchids) to flowers of radial symmetry (as in the daisy). Mutation of the *CYCLOIDEA* gene of snapdragon has this effect. So a character such as floral symmetry, which might in itself be considered the product of the differential action of hundreds or thousands of genes, can in fact be switched by a single gene. Similarly, the complexity of floral pattern in roses, with multiple layers of petals, can be generated in the simple Arabidopsis flower by a single mutation, in the *AGAMOUS* gene. In the same species, the activation, rather than inactivation, of the *KNAT1* gene converts the usual simple leaf shape into a lobed leaf typical of other species. And entire biochemical pathways of pigment, oil or starch production can be triggered in tissues that don't normally accumulate them by activating single genes. The genes in these examples are molecular switches at the top of cascades, to activate entire programmes of development or biochemical synthesis.

> plants are central to helping solve the problems facing mankind

Evolution can act on these genes to effect large changes in plant morphology and biochemistry in simple steps, rather than as a series of very many small, incremental changes. Plant breeders could achieve major crop improvements in a more directed way, if they have the information on which genes control specific characters. Breeders have selected for such characters in the past, in the absence of information on gene sequences, but the future allows greater precision, as crop genomes are sequenced.

Genes, and their interactions with the environment, make the difference between species, between tissues, between crop success and failure. The Earth's environment is changing, and so is our ability to control gene flow between species. The next big issue for society is how we manage both.

Casson, S. A., Lindsey, K. (2006) 'The *turnip* mutant of *Arabidopsis* reveals that *LEC1* expression mediates the effects of auxin and sugars to promote embryonic cell identity', *Plant Physiology* 142: 526–41

House of Lords European Union Committee (2006), *The EU Strategy on Biofuels; from field to fuel* 47th Report. London: HMSO

Royal Society report on Non-food Crops (1999): available via *http://www.royalsoc.ac.uk*

Humans and animals

Christopher Rowe

THERE ARE TWO MODELS of human nature represented in Plato's dialogues, one familiar, and ultimately pessimistic, one more optimistic – and less familiar to our ears. According to the first model, every human being is by nature a locus of conflict, between reason, on the one hand, and irrational desire on the other. Reason is perpetually under threat from desire, or passion (our 'animal' impulses). According to the second, less familiar, model, our desires are always aimed at what is really best for us; our problem is with establishing what *is* best for us. Desire, on this account, can do no wrong, and it is our reason(ing) that leads us astray. Given Plato's conviction, in accord with the second model, that the nature of the human good, and of the good in general, is something discoverable by human reason, our primary need – if we are to achieve the good life that we all desire, even while not knowing what it actually is – will be to train our rational faculties: to become *philosophers*, and to seek the truth. According to the first model, by contrast, the primary requirement of a satisfactory life will be the training of the passions, which if uncontrolled will tend to crowd out the demands and potentialities of reason, leaving us increasingly indistinguishable from lower animals. Indeed from this perspective our humanity itself is something we have to struggle to maintain, perhaps even to achieve. But if we all, always, desire what is good (and the good is the beautiful, the ordered and the harmonious), then human

> by nature, is every human being a locus of conflict?

beings will be fully human from the beginning, and through and through.

This latter, optimistic, perspective – the second model – is generally associated with Socrates, Plato's teacher; and on the standard interpretation there is a defining moment when Plato does the sensible thing and rejects his teacher's view. Yet, as I argue in a new book, there is clear evidence that Plato retains the Socratic model of humanity alongside the 'Platonic'. The Socratic picture represents what we essentially are. The apparently rival, 'Platonic', one is merely a picture of what we tend to *become*, as a result of allowing ourselves – because it always is, or was, something we could have avoided, if we had been sufficiently on our guard – to develop too great an interest in the wrong things (things that are not really good for us, things we do not *really* want). The result is that we come to think we cannot help ourselves, but that view, Plato wants to say, is an example of our own lack of self-knowledge. Radical measures may now be necessary, but it need not be, or need not have been, like that.

The Socratic position, as developed by Plato, is – when properly grasped – philosophically robust. Both it and its Platonic version have profound implications for the way we understand ourselves and others, for our educational priorities, and for the living of life itself.

Penner, T. and Rowe, C. (2005) *Plato's Lysis*. Cambridge: Cambridge University Press

Plato: Complete Works (1996): see especially *Lysis, Phaedo, Republic IV and X*. Indianapolis: Hackett

Rowe, C. (2007) *Plato and the Art of Philosophical Writing*. Cambridge: Cambridge University Press

Talking rubbish

John Chapman

ONE OF THE DEFINING CHARACTERISTICS of modern humans is our consistent and massive production of rubbish. There is no end to the mountains of rubbish that defile otherwise beautiful cultural landscapes and few communities are now prepared to accept the rubbish of their neighbours. Despite more widespread sorting, recycling and treatment, the monumental nature of our rubbish production is unique among species. Small wonder, then, that we rarely step back from the mountains of garbage, from debates over recycling and how to improve tip maintenance, and try to understand refuse in terms of its cultural meanings. A comparative world history of rubbish would be a particularly illuminating exercise.

> the monumental nature of our rubbish production is unique among species

Richard Gould's claim that 'residue behaviour, like language, is universal to man' supports a foundation narrative for the discipline of archaeology, whose primary concern is with the rubbish of past generations. Yet this origin myth is potentially misleading. It imposes on the past a modern Euro-American view of rubbish as something once active which should be segregated from the processes of the living, for health or ideological reasons. The dangers in transferring these assumptions to past practices are twofold. First, they increase the distance between 'dead rubbish' and once-living people, making it harder to interpret the connections between them. Secondly, they drastically reduce ways of understanding deposition, since refuse disposal can hardly be anything but unproblematic and unso-phisticated. The category of 'rubbish' is, then, just as historic-ally constituted as the term 'society'.

There have been two major conversations about rubbish over the last twenty years – one between archaeologists and the other among sociologists (and anthropologists). For the most part, archaeologists have sought to understand how sites, as concentrations of refuse, were created. Less well developed is the minority view of the structured ways in which people treated refuse, ways that shed light on the symbolic order of past communities.

For sociologists such as Kevin Hetherington, the disposal of dirt, as matter out of place, is about the agency of the absent – what waste can do even when removed from society. Waste disposal is thus an important practice in maintaining cultural order – the treatment of waste helps a society to make sense of itself. Thompson has even suggested that the three categories of the transient, the durable and rubbish permitted the uneven distribution of social power and status in our society, forming the basis for cultural differences between classes. But sociologi-cal attempts to define categories of rubbish and their conduits of disposal have consistently overlooked the archaeological dimension.

While these two conversations have taken place in splendid dis-ciplinary isolation, it is clear that a dialogue would illuminate the cultural significance of rubbish. Understanding more about where rubbish comes from (culturally) should make a differ-ence to where it goes (practically). In this sense, talking rubbish could pay handsome dividends both for our global ecologies and for our local cultural understanding of ourselves.

Hetherington, K. (2004) 'Secondhandedness: consumption, disposal and absent presence', *Environment and Planning D: Space and Society* 22: 157–73

Schiffer, M. B. (1987) *Formation Processes of the Archaeological Record.* Albuquerque: University of New Mexico Press

Thompson, M. (1979) *Rubbish Theory. The creation and destruction of value.* Oxford: Oxford University Press

The Earth's DNA

Jon Davidson

NATURAL PROCESSES THAT CONTROL large-scale phenomena are recorded in tiny archives – the crystals in a rock
and the layers of a stalactite or a tooth. As in most sciences
there is a continuum of scales of observation in earth sciences.
Just as nuclear physics helps us to understand the cosmos,
understanding phenomena at the smallest scales is critical to
appreciating larger-scale global processes. The earth sciences
community has pioneered the analysis of natural materials for
their elemental and isotopic compositions, and has progressively reduced the scale at which they can be observed. We
now use tiny drills in clean laboratories, laser beams and ion
beams to target microscopic samples. We can now take com-
positional profiles across tiny crystals from magmas, which
help us to understand how the magma evolved, and over what
timescales. This approach is analogous to 'reading' tree rings
to determine the history of the changing environment in which
the tree grew. We can analyse the isotopic compositions of
mineral grains less than 1mm across which 'remember' the
times in which they were formed, and hence determine the
growth history of the continental crust, and the episodic record
of crust extraction from the mantle. We can analyse composi-
tional gradients in crystals to determine the timescales of the
processes which affect them as they grow, and have seen evidence for events in single crystals that may be associated with
other natural phenomena, such as earthquakes. We can even
analyse tiny aliquots of fluids or melts trapped in minerals (less
than a millionth of a gram) to tell us about crystallisation

conditions (pressures, temperatures) at the time when they formed.

Like crystals, corals, carbonate dripstones in caves and glacial ice grow by progressive deposition of layers, with the composition of the layer reflecting that of the water from which it is precipitated. We can reconstruct past climates by determining the isotopic composition of oxygen and carbon in layers from stalactites, corals or glacial ice. We can similarly analyse single bird feathers for isotopic compositions to ascertain their origin and migration paths – a very useful tool in light of recent worries over the spread of bird flu. Beyond the realm of rocks and minerals, we can analyse tiny amounts of archaeological artefacts or skeletal remains to determine where they came from. The isotopic compositions of teeth can tell us about the climate in which individuals lived, and their diets, and changes in such conditions determined by tracing growth zones can be related to population migrations. The isotopic compositions of artefacts, such as those containing lead, can be used to trace trade routes. Our challenge will be to devise even more applications to keep up with these capabilities.

Jerram, D. A. and Davidson, J. P. (eds.) (2007) 'Frontiers in Textural and Microgeochemical Analysis', *Elements* 3: 4

Cosmic dark thoughts

Carlos Frenk

COSMOLOGY CONFRONTS some of the most fundamental questions in the whole of science, many of which have preoccupied humankind since the beginning of civilisation: How and when did our universe begin? What is it made of? How did it acquire its current appearance? Theoretical and observational research over the past twenty-five years has begun to provide answers to some of these questions and these are encapsulated in the standard model of cosmology, in whose development Durham cosmologists have played a leading role over the past two decades. This model agrees with a staggering amount of astronomical data, from the observed properties of the heat left over from the Big Bang to the complex web-like clustering pattern of galaxies. Yet the standard model of cosmology raises a number of profound questions which have no immediate answer within the current framework of physics. This has led some theoretical physicists to argue that certain properties of our universe cannot be understood at a fundamental level, but rather that things are the way they are because otherwise life would have not been able to emerge. I believe that this view is fundamentally flawed and that the traditional scientific method upon which physics has flourished will deliver a rational explanation for those properties of our universe that, today, seem to us bizarre.

The most perplexing aspect of our universe is the presence of a form of energy of 'empty space', the dark energy, which currently makes up the bulk of the universe and is causing its expansion to accelerate. There is no explanation for the dark energy, even though Einstein introduced a related concept, the cosmological constant, into his equations of general relativity in a misguided attempt to explain why, prior to Hubble's discovery of the cosmic expansion, the universe seemed to be static. There are now a number of compelling lines of empirical evidence for the existence of dark energy, including a particularly convincing one provided by cosmologists at Durham and their international collaborators. Although it provides the bulk of the material content of our universe, the dark energy is 10^{120} smaller than the 'natural' value expected from the known laws of physics. It is this dramatic failure that has led to the anthropic explanation for the existence of dark energy.

In its most seductive form, the anthropic argument is cast within the proposal that our 'universe' is not unique and that, in fact, there exists a very large ensemble of distinct worlds, the 'multiverse', in which the laws of physics and the values of the fundamental constants of nature (such as Newton's constant) can differ. Only particular forms of these laws and specific values of these constants allow a long-lived universe in

'empty space' is the most perplexing aspect of our universe

which the conditions for life are realised; evidently ours is one of these worlds. There is therefore no fundamental explanation for the existence of dark energy – without it (or with too much of it) we would just not be here. The idea of the multiverse fits in naturally within 'string theory', an elegant, currently fashionable attempt to provide a unified description of quantum and gravitational phenomena. A 'landscape' of worlds is readily accommodated within this description. String theory is speculative and has so far failed to generate a single prediction that can be tested experimentally. The ability to make testable predictions lies at the heart of science and it is this that distinguishes physics from other forms of intellectual endeavour. A second basic tenet of physics is that all natural phenomena can be explained as manifestations of a set of simple, fundamental laws that are universal. String theory may turn out to be correct (only experiment will tell) and the multiverse may indeed exist. However, there must be a rational explanation, rooted in the laws of physics, for the existence and properties of this most puzzling of cosmic phenomena, the dark energy. It may well be that this explanation will require a fundamental revision of the currently known laws of physics. Finding it is one of the great challenges of twenty-first-century science.

Frenk, C. S. (2002) 'Simulating the formation of cosmic structure', *Philosophical transactions of the Royal Society* 360: 1277

Springel, V., Frenk, C. S. and White, S. D. M. (2006) 'The large-scale structure of the Universe', *Nature* 440: 1137–44

Susskind, L. (2005) *The Cosmic Landscape: String Theory and the illusion of intelligent design.* London: Little Brown

Where does mass come from?

Nigel Glover

THE STANDARD MODEL of particle physics is the theory that describes the tiny building-blocks of the universe. It is widely recognised as one of the biggest achievements in twentieth-century science. It says that everything around us is made of microscopic fundamental particles called quarks and leptons that interact via four kinds of forces.

We are most familiar with the forces of electromagnetism and gravity, but the other two are less known. The strong nuclear force binds atomic nuclei together, rendering them stable and long-lived. Without it, there would be no atoms other than hydrogen, and therefore no planets and no life. The weak nuclear force is responsible for the nuclear reactions that cause the sun to shine. As a result, billions of neutrinos from the sun go through our body every second. Luckily we don't feel them, precisely because the weak force is so incredibly weak.

> billions of neutrinos go through our body every second

Despite its many successes, the Standard Model has some serious problems. For example, it says all of the elementary particles are massless and, according to Einstein's theory of special relativity, travel at the speed of light – just like the photon. Massive particles can never reach light-speed. However, experiments tell us unambiguously that most elementary particles do actually have mass. The key question for particle physicists is: 'How do the masses of the elementary particles arise?'

Well, we are still not sure exactly how particles get their mass. Since the 1960s, the prevailing idea is that particles gain mass by interacting with a field which permeates the universe – the Higgs Field. This field can slow down some (otherwise massless) elementary particles, so that they behave like massive particles travelling at less than light-speed. The more strongly a particle interacts with this field, the greater its mass and the slower it travels.

Of course the photon is immune to the field: and therefore does not slow down and remains massless. The Higgs field itself is not directly measurable but it does produce observable effects. High-energy accelerators might be able to excite the Higgs field and create 'Higgs bosons' that could leave detectable traces in enormous detectors built exactly for that purpose.

So far, experiments using the world's most powerful accelerators have not observed any Higgs bosons, but indirect experimental evidence suggests that particle physicists are poised for a profound discovery. The Large Hadron Collider (LHC) in Europe (at CERN), switched on in the autumn of 2008, is expected to start colliding protons travelling at speeds close to the speed of light with energies seven times higher than any previous man-made accelerator.

Higgs, P. W. (1964) 'Broken Symmetries and the Masses of Gauge Bosons', *Physical Review Letters* 13: 508–509

Lederman, L. (1993) *The God Particle: If the universe is the answer, what is the question?*. New York: Houghton Mifflin Co.

The material economy and the question of 'waste'

Ray Hudson

WHAT IS 'THE ECONOMY' if not the process of working on various forms of materials in order to create wealth, prosperity and well-being? Social scientists have studied the economy in terms of the creation of values, the creation of meanings, and the location of economic value in everyday cultural practice.

In contrast, material scientists have understood the economy as a series of transformations governed by the laws of thermodynamics, emphasising the changes in the chemical and physical composition of matter as materials are fashioned to become useful artefacts. However, whereas social scientific approaches have typically ignored the materiality of the economy, material science approaches have turned a blind eye to the socio-economics of the economy. What is needed is a synthesis of the concerns of material and social science.

Such a synthesis would draw attention to the economy as a series of material transformations; involving artefacts as things socially shaped and situated in time and space. This perspective contests and rejects the myth of the economy governed by unchanging laws. At the same time it emphasises that these transformations are accomplished by human labour, and recognises that they always have unintended as well as intended outcomes. It prompts to think of 'waste' as something that is produced at every step in the material economy and not something that emerges as the residue of a linear process.

Rather than think in terms of the disposal of 'wastes', we need to think in terms of the continuous reshaping of matter between various socially useful states. Consider, for example, the boom in car boot sales as things that have become surplus to the requirements of some are sold on precisely because they are seen as useful to others, for a variety of reasons ranging from bare economics to an ethical concern for the world around us. Moreover, there needs to be recognition that the definition of 'waste' is also one that is culturally situated – what is 'waste' in one cultural context may become a valuable resource in another. Consider, for example, some of the ships that have reached the end of their socially useful and insurable lives in the EU and are then driven onto beaches in Bangladesh. There they become a veritable repository of varied artefacts and materials, deconstructed from being 'a ship' into component materials and parts, virtually every scrap of which is used as a resource in one way or another.

Callon, M., Méadel, C. and Rabeharisoa, V. (2002) 'The economy of qualities', *Economy and Society* 31: 194–217

Georgescu-Roegen, N. (1971) *The Entropy Law and the Economic Process.* Cambridge: Cambridge University Press

Sum, N.-L. and Jessop, B. (2007) *Towards a Cultural Political Economy.* Cheltenham: Edward Elgar

Quantum entanglement

Ifan Hughes

THE MOST MYSTERIOUS FEATURE of quantum mechanics is entanglement – the property that the quantum states of two things which once interacted cannot be treated individually, rather the system must be considered as one entity, even if the objects are spatially separated by vast distances. The strong correlation between separated systems undermines the belief in an objective reality independent of measurement.

Correlations are a common feature of the world. If a pair of gloves is in a drawer, and one is removed to a distant location, someone finding a left glove in the drawer predicts with certainty that the removed glove is right-handed. On looking into the drawer our information changes. Whereas quantum entanglement requires correlation, correlated systems are not necessarily entangled. The counter-intuitive nature of entanglement was highlighted by Einstein and colleagues in 1935. The thought experiment proposed by Einstein – a founder of quantum mechanics who remained unreconciled to its fundamental probabilistic nature – was designed to illustrate the strangest aspect of quantum theory, which he referred to as 'spooky action at a distance'. The ideological debate raged through the second half of the last century, but two exciting recent developments are that these ideas can now be tested by physicists in laboratories, and it has been recognised that entanglement is a resource.

> correlations are a common feature of the world

There are no everyday examples of 'spooky action at a distance'

– it is a feature of the quantum world, only revealed through the behaviour of individual quantum entities like atoms and photons. Nevertheless, quantum entanglement will be employed to realise new technologies such as quantum cryptography, teleportation and computing. Whereas the computing speed of a classical computer might double if twice as many bits are available to store information, for so-called quantum computers there is an exponential gain in speed afforded by entangling quantum bits. However, exploiting entangled states necessitates the production and manipulation of quantum entanglement in a controlled and flexible way.

The biggest hurdle to overcome is that entangled states are very quickly destroyed by interactions with the external world. Current experiments aim to produce entangled states in an isolated environment where they will survive for a long time. This will enable the manipulation of entangled states and establish the building blocks of a new generation of powerful computers exploiting entanglement. The method involves lasers to cool atoms to a millionth of a degree above absolute zero. At these very low temperatures it is possible to trap atoms using laser beams and form crystals of ultra-cold atoms bound by light. To create entanglement, atoms in the lattice must interact with one another. Such an interaction can be mediated by using a laser pulse. In addition to the technologically exciting prospects for the advancement of computing, in the next few years physicists will further enhance their understanding of the fundamental nature of the quantum world.

Einstein, A., Podolsky, B. and Rosen, N. (1935) 'Can quantum-mechanical description of physical reality be considered complete?' *Physical Review* 47: 77–80

Haroche, S. and Raimond, J.-M. (2006) *Exploring the Quantum.* Oxford: Oxford University Press.

Nielson, M. A. and Chuang, I. L. (2000) *Quantum Computation and Quantum Information.* Cambridge: Cambridge University Press

Extra space-time dimensions

James Stirling

THE QUESTION of how many dimensions we live in is fundamental, but surprisingly it remains unresolved. Our everyday experience is of course of four dimensions (three space plus one time) but in the last few decades attempts by theoretical particle physicists to construct a 'theory of everything' for the nature and properties of the fundamental particles and forces, including gravity, have led to the conclusion that there may be a large number of *additional* space-time dimensions, that have so far remained hidden from observation.

The behaviour of objects under the force of gravity is described by Einstein's general theory of relativity. Gravity is the only one of the four fundamental forces that is relevant in the macroscopic world of people, planets and galaxies. The other three forces (the strong, electromagnetic and weak forces) are only relevant in the sub-atomic quantum world inhabited by the fundamental particles, the quarks and leptons, which make up all matter in the universe. Throughout the twentieth century, much effort was devoted to finding a 'quantum' theory of gravity that would apply also to the microscopic world and would open up the possibility of unifying all four forces in a single theory.

Extra space-time dimensions are a feature of the main, and indeed currently the only, contender for the theory of quantum gravity, string theory. String theory is only mathematically consistent in 10 or 11 dimensions, and so the idea that there are extra dimensions that are rolled up or 'compactified', and hence not readily observed, seems natural. Although string theory does not yet seem to indicate how large these extra dimensions might be, it was until recently assumed that they must be extremely tiny and that any new gravitational effects associated with the new extra-dimension theory would consequently be too small to be observed.

However, in recent years theoretical particle physicists have discovered that the scale of the additional (6 or 7) dimensions may be much larger than previously thought, so that they may give rise to observable phenomena at the next generation of high-energy particle colliders.

In one version of the extra-dimensions theory, three of the fundamental forces (strong, weak, electromagnetic) are confined to 3+1 dimensional 'membranes', whereas the fourth, gravity, operates in the entire higher-dimensional volume, thus allowing it to feel the effects of extra dimensions.

And if the extra dimensions are sufficiently large, then the laws of gravity could be modified at distances that, although still tiny, may be within reach of experiment. For example, when fundamental particles are made to collide, the effects of the gravitational interaction between them are normally swamped by those of the other three forces. However in the extra-dimension theory, the gravitational interaction is greatly enhanced if the colliding particles have sufficiently high energy.

the idea that there are extra dimensions seems natural

The latest and most powerful particle collider, the Large Hadron Collider at the CERN Laboratory in Geneva, Switzerland, came into operation in 2008. It will collide two beams of protons at very high energy, and scientists will study the way in which the fundamental constituents of each proton (the quarks and gluons) interact. The way in which the energetic constituents of one colliding proton scatter off those in the other proton could be influenced by new gravitational effects associated with the extra dimension theory, and so a detailed comparison of what is expected in the standard version of the theory with what is observed may provide the first evidence of this new type of physics.

The experimental discovery of large extra dimensions would potentially be a Nobel Prize-winning achievement.

Arkani-Hamed, N., Dimopoulos. S. and Dvali, G. (1998) 'The Hierarchy Problem and New Dimensions at a Millimetre', *Physics Letters* B429: 263–72

Greene, B. (2004) *The Elegant Universe: Superstrings, hidden dimensions, and the quest for the ultimate theory,* new edn. New York: Norton.

Climate change in the rocks

Maurice Tucker

SEDIMENTARY ROCK is one of the most fundamental elements of the geological record, the significance of which was recognised by James Hutton in the eighteenth century. Bedding is a characteristic feature of sedimentary rock and the question to be asked is, 'What is its origin?'

New work on Carboniferous limestone in Weardale and Teesdale in the Pennines shows that the occurrence of the beds is not random; they show patterns in their bed thickness – they get thinner and thicker upwards. The beds, which consist of fossiliferous limestone separated by muddy layers, are also laterally extensive: you can follow individual beds of rock just 20 centimetres thick over the whole of the northern Pennines, an area of 10,000 square kilometres. So beds are distinct and they are organised into packages. Trace elements and stable isotopes also display systematic variations through the limestones. Similar patterns in beds have also been found in Permian and Jurassic limestones; in fact, they are ubiquitous. Of particular note is that the beds were deposited on a millennial time-scale, each bed representing around 1–3,000 years.

> beds are distinct and organised into packages

Some natural processes, like changes in climate, were clearly controlling the deposition of the beds and these were varying regularly. The most likely explanation is that the beds are the result of alternations of wetter and drier periods. Clay would have been washed in during wetter periods and more limestone precipitated during warmer, arid times. And when you start looking at sedimentary rocks of different ages, you find that there are patterns in the beds everywhere. This discovery has enormous significance.

It would appear that there have been subtle but regular changes in climate throughout the geological record, fluctuations in aridity and humidity, and the evidence is there in the basic element of the sedimentary record – the beds of rock. Millennial-scale climatic changes are well known in the Quaternary, the most recent geological period of the last few million years, but the suggestion here is that such changes go much further back in time. Regular, systematic and persistent fluctuations in carbonate precipitation and clay input can only be explained in terms of variations in solar output, causing changes in temperature and humidity. Beds of limestone provide evidence of regular fluctuations in solar output on a millennial scale. This is a matter of great significance in these days of debate over climate change.

Sarntheim, M. et al. (2002) 'Decadal to millennial-scale climate variability – chronology and mechanisms', *Quaternary Science Reviews* 21: 1121–28

Wilson, R. C. L. et al. (2000) *The Great Ice Age: Climate change and life*. London and New York: Open University and Routledge

The urban condition

Ash Amin

THE HUMAN CONDITION has become the urban condition. In 1950, one-third of the world's population lived in cities, but by 2050 the figure is expected to rise to two-thirds, or 6 billion people. By 2015 each of the world's ten largest cities will house between 20 million and 30 million people. Arguably, even those people who are not included in these figures now owe much of their existence to the demands that cities place on the world economy. And these people are increasingly drawn into the urban orbit too, as cities incorporate edge settlements, shanty towns and commuter zones, and shape the content of televisions, computers and software-aided devices which cut deep into the countryside and beyond. The urban footprint is ubiquitous. It forces radical rethinking, firstly of the whereabouts of the urban, and secondly, of the signature of the urban on the human condition.

> cities function as the collecting points of life

Turning to the first question, we have become used to the idea of cities as territorially bounded spaces of varying density and spread, which at some point fade into the rural or somewhere else. This idea allows us to imagine – frequently hark back to – a rural hinterland and a different, slower, perhaps more wholesome way of life. It allows us to imagine city life as territorially demarcated, motored by its own internal dynamic and decidedly modern, fast, and fragmented. But ubiquitous urbanisation – manifest in urban sprawl, the overnight appearance of refugee settlements in the middle of nowhere, the urban out-pourings of signs, people and goods cutting across the land-scape and linking life in one place to that in faraway places – challenges the image of terrestrial space as a patchwork of cities and countrysides. It requires an imagination of cities as a meshwork, a topological surface of interconnected nodes, lines and voids, allowing visualisation of cities as stretched, porous and relationally constituted spatial forms. Cities function as the collecting points of life manifest in diverse spatial forms, from juxtaposed streets and buildings to transnational communica-tion and trade networks. London, Luanda, and Leipzig are in each other and elsewhere, and traversed or haunted by many distant entities and actors.

To see the urban condition in this way, secondly, requires a shift in perspective on the human condition. Ubiquitous urban-isation implies that it is not possible to think the contemporary human condition through anything other than an urban optic. This is not just a matter of noting the connections between humans in different places; their meshwork composition. Nor is it just a matter of questioning the difference between city folk and country folk or between the urban and rural way of life. It is, above all, a matter of recognising the formative influence of ubiquitous urbanism on contemporary modes of human being. The precise details of this influence are far from clear, but it includes the instinct of adaptation to multiple sensory, techno-logical and environmental inputs, the call to inhabit many time-spaces of dwelling, meaning and community, and the habit of negotiating a world fully revealed, with all its risks and opportunities, delights and disenchantments. These might be some of the emerging measures of being modern in the hyper-urban age.

As such, they do not anticipate a chameleon-like or cyborg human, roaming the world unperturbed by the inflections of place and circumstance. This is a creature that inhabits only the worst kinds of fiction. Instead, they signal future imperative, a trace of what will be, what modern living demands. Even if they fall short of touching life in all places in the same way, still allowing different experiences of the urban way of being among different people in different locations, they cannot be ignored. They come with an injunction that cautions against rural escape and nostalgia, against seeing the urban way of life as extraordinary or devilish, and against ignoring the urban in future projections, from government plans on economy, politics and society, to models of human progress and emancipation.

Amin, A. and Thrift, N. (2002) *Cities: Reimagining the Urban.* Cambridge: Polity Press

Tonkiss, F. (2005) *Space, the City and Social Theory.* Cambridge: Polity Press

Wirth, L. (1964) *Urbanism as a Way of Life.* Chicago: University of Chicago Press

Will the West Antarctic Ice Sheet collapse?

Mike Bentley

THERE IS A FAMILIAR CLIMATE CHANGE mantra that if the West Antarctic Ice Sheet collapses then it will cause 5 metres of global sea level rise. In terms of the challenges facing our society this ranks up there as one of the biggest – 100 million people live within 1 metre of sea level and so we face the prospect of tens of millions of refugees, and trillions of dollars of asset damage world-wide. But the critical word in that mantra is 'if'. Are we actually any closer to knowing if the West Antarctic Ice Sheet (WAIS) *will* collapse or what conditions would cause collapse? In other words, how warm do the air and ocean have to get over and around Antarctica before we are sure that the ice sheet will melt or slough the majority of its mass into the ocean? Could it even be happening already? Has it ever happened before, millions of years ago in the geological past, and, if so, what can we learn from past events about how it will happen and what might be the early warning signs?

> 100 million people live within 1 metre of sea level

These are questions that drive much of the ice sheet research in Durham's geography department, working in collaboration with scientists at British Antarctic Survey and abroad. Have we made any progress in answering them? The answer is an emphatic yes. The last few years have seen enormous advances in our understanding of how the ice sheet works. We now know that rather than being the somewhat inert lump of ice it was thought to be, slow to react to any external change, the WAIS actually responds on very short timescales: ice streams can speed up and slow down during a single tidal cycle, ice shelves can disappear in just a few weeks, and large lakes beneath the ice fill and empty in less than a month. Moreover, we have discovered that different sectors of the WAIS have been responding in markedly different ways. A key area of our involvement has been in highlighting ice sheet behaviour over the last few millennia. This is important because it not only gives us a long-term 'trajectory' of change, but shows us by what mechanisms and how fast the ice sheet has changed in the past – what it is 'capable of'. It also provides badly needed hard data against which models can be tested. Ice sheet models are like weather-forecasting models – they have to be trialled against past data to see if they correctly simulate the natural world. In the parlance this is known as 'hindcasting'. Only when a model can properly hindcast a wide range of past behaviour can it be used to forecast what the ice sheet might do in a future climate.

Ice sheet models cannot yet do this reliably, although they're substantially better than a decade ago. We face some tricky scientific challenges – most requiring expensive investigations in Antarctica – before our predictive abilities are reliable enough to inform policy makers. The eventual aim must be to develop the computer models to the point where we can remove uncertainty – to determine reliably whether the 'if' in that mantra about WAIS collapse should be replaced by 'when', or in fact whether we think the ice sheet will be a robust feature in a warmer world.

Mercer, J. H. (1976) 'West Antarctic Ice Sheet and CO_2 greenhouse effect: a threat of disaster', *Nature* 271: 321–25

Oppenheimer, M. (1998) 'Global warming and the stability of the West Antarctic Ice Sheet', *Nature* 393: 325–32

Vaughan, D. G. (2008) 'West Antarctic Ice Sheet collapse – the fall and rise of a paradigm', *Climatic Change* 91: 65–79

Images and humanitarianism

David Campbell

EVERYDAY LIFE IN WORLD POLITICS is replete with images and policy makers are attuned to their power. Speaking at the World Press Photo 50th anniversary in 2005, the UN Secretary General's special representative for Sudan called on photojournalists to produce more pictures as part of the struggle for attention and action in Darfur. In making this statement, Jan Pronk recognised that, although most people get their news from television, the still photograph remains a powerful medium through which we become attuned to others and the processes of de-humanisation that some are subjected to.

As genres, documentary photography and photojournalism have historically been humanitarian technologies. For example, they played a notable role in nineteenth-century labour reforms, the New Deal policies of the 1930s and the coverage of conflict in the post-Second World War period. Today, however, these photographic genres are the central technology of humanitarianism. The photographic image now has a primary role in establishing the mediated conditions of possibility for our engagement with, and possible response to, the suffering of others.

we have come to rely on stereotypical icons of disaster

Historically, photography has produced contradictory effects in its effort to sustain humanness. In relation to 'Africa' – so often the homogenised site for a visual humanitarianism – the well-known portrayals of the crisis in Biafra, the famine in Ethiopia, genocide in Rwanda, HIV/AIDS in the sub-Saharan region, and violence in Darfur that dominate reportage from the continent have merged into a dystopic portrait. Pictures of passive women and children, helpless victims in the face of large forces, are continually reproduced in an effort to get our attention and force action. Yet the portraits of pity that lead many to donate generously in response to charity appeals also reinforce colonial and racial stereotypes. They hinder our ethical engagement with others, keeping difference at a distance.

Moving beyond this dilemma in pursuit of a better way of visualising de-humanisation has to avoid the iconoclastic critique that W. J. T. Mitchell regards as falsely revelling in the view that 'the destruction or exposure of false images amounts to a political victory' (2002: 175). That is because the problem is not so much the *presence* of such imagery – it would be foolish to deny the reality of the abuses that documentary photography and photojournalism have recorded over time – but, rather, the *absence* of other views amongst the pictures transmitted to us as citizen viewers.

We have to ask those responsible for bringing us the photographs – from the photojournalists, to their agencies, the picture editors, and media outlets that make up the global visual economy – how we have come to rely on stereotypical icons of disaster to illustrate stories of complex political emergencies. Above all else, we have to investigate other ways of witnessing the many processes of de-humanisation that currently mark our political condition. The solution to this will not be purely photographic – because in the end all media are mixed media – but the solution will be one in which documentary photography and photojournalism have a pivotal role to play.

Mitchell, W. J. T. (2002), 'Showing Seeing: A critique of visual culture', *Journal of Visual Culture* 1 (2): 165–81

Schwartz, J. and Ryan, J. (eds.) (2003) *Picturing Place: Photography and the geographical imagination*. London: I. B. Tauris

Sontag, S. (2004) *On Regarding the Pain of Others*. New York: Picador

Terror

Stephen Graham

FEW WORDS are as ubiquitous in media and political commentary these days as 'terror' and 'terrorism'. Fewer still are so charged with controversy and so elusive when it comes to precise definition.

In the context of a globe-stretching programme of war and political violence, emanating from the US and UK governments, amongst other nations, to allegedly target 'terrorism', the stakes in defining these terms could hardly be higher. Because this 'war' targets a style of political violence, it has few geographical limits and no obvious end-point. Worryingly, it also offers all manner of dubious regimes around the world an opportunity to ride on its coat tails in clamping down on

> the 'war on terror' has few geographical limits and no obvious end-point

dissent and ratcheting up repression. Generally, the 'war on terror' has led to a major global 'chill' on democratic dissent, as often legitimate political activities come under the gaze of extending state 'counter-terror' laws.

In many places, new counter-terror state campaigns are targeting indigenous people campaigning for their human rights as well as Islamist or other groups prone to commit spectacular acts of violence against civilians or symbolic targets. In many places, political and ecological activists, and anti-military or anti-globalisation campaigners have also been widely targeted in counter-terror legislation. Frequently, this has radically delegitimised often legitimate causes and allowed new state policies to undermine legitimate rights of dissent built up over centuries of democratic activism at a stroke. Who, after all, is likely to publicly support activities widely labelled as 'terrorism'?

Such labelling sustains what the Italian philosopher Giorgio Agamben has called a state of exception. This is the idea that, because terrorist actions are deemed to be existential threats to whole societies, emergency measures are required which very often sediment out into more or less permanent transformations of law or geography. The law thus has the power to suspend itself.

In the 'global war on terror', for example, long-standing laws of international humanitarian protection, human rights and criminal prosecution have been widely abandoned or side-stepped. New spaces of perpetual incarceration without trial have emerged for those 'illegal combatants' hoovered up in the various military campaigns. These are based in a global archipelago of camps and enclaves which form a legal and geographical no man's land across the world, both within and beyond the formal geographies of states. In addition, with media complicity, citizens labelled 'terrorist' or 'terrorist sympathiser' have been depicted as shadowy threats, who, stripped of their human rights, can be attacked or incarcerated at will, in *anticipation* of their possible threat, as a pre-emptive defence of 'freedom'.

In contrast with such manipulative rhetoric, a more accurate definition of terrorism is that it involves political violence deliberately launched against civilians or civilian targets for the purposes of instilling fear, transmitting a symbolic message, undermining the political power of a purported enemy, or pursuing a political or geopolitical agenda. This definition means that violence by non-state fighters against the occupying military forces of a foreign power is not best described as terrorism.

Agamben, G. (2005) *The State of Exception*. Chicago: University of Chicago Press

Graham, S. (2004) *Cities, War and Terrorism*. Oxford: Blackwell

Zulaika, J. and Douglass, W. (1996) *Terror and Taboo*. New York: Routledge

The stateless African society

Reuben Loffman

WHILST A STATELESS AFRICAN SOCIETY might, in the short term, be confined to being a fairly abstract intellectual entity, it is still an idea worth pursuing in the wake of chronic state failure in Africa. Moreover, certain theoretical features of a stateless society, such as the more frequent use of customary law, could still be integrated within existing state systems. The ontology of a stateless African society, however, cannot be monolithic. Stateless societies in Africa have taken, and may take, multifarious forms. Nevertheless, there are some features that could be common to all future stateless societies.

Firstly, governmental power is always decentralised in a stateless society – and this would certainly be the case with this idea. Rather than being run from a metropolis, therefore, small polities would congregate over certain geographic areas. Free of a centralised government system, African people could exert more political agency over smaller communities numbering in the hundreds and not the millions. This would be an extreme form of proportional representation, then, whereby the 'proportions' would actually be politically independent from any centre. Additionally, these polities could organise economies and legislation through technologies, such as the internet and the mobile telephone, which are already in widespread use in Africa.

Secondly, the idea of decentralised polities has legal benefits too. Rather than being defined by intransigent legal codes, which are all too often artefacts of arbitrary colonial rule, stateless societies in Africa could turn more to customary law. This approach has very real practical advantages. In the Democratic Republic of the Congo, for instance, customary law has often proved flexible enough to settle land disputes after fighting has subsided.

Lastly, there are many economic approaches open to any potential stateless society. However, market anarchism, or the belief that voluntary free-market relationships should replace state-coerced relations, could provide the best economic underpinning for small, decentralised, African polities. Already the informal – and unregulated – economy in Africa provides a living for millions of people. As such, market anarchism would be an organic way to organise stateless African economies. This market system would concurrently differentiate the small polities outlined here from being anarcho-syndicalist, a stateless model which would not recognise private property. Without recognition of private property, Africa could alienate itself still further from global capital. However, market anarchism could integrate Africa more efficiently into capitalist-led world markets by freeing African agents from state regulation whilst simultaneously recognising private property. Moreover, market anarchism could provide some basis for collective action if situated within the social and technical frameworks of the polities and technologies outlined above. In sum, then, stateless societies could help African people to accumulate wealth as well as to resolve conflicts.

Davidson, B. (1992) *The Black Man's Burden: Africa and the curse of the nation-state*. New York: James Currey

Nest, M., Grignon, F., Kisangani, E. F. (2006) *The Democratic Republic of the Congo: Economic dimensions of war and peace*. Boulder, CO and London: Lynne Rienner

Nozick, R. (1974) *Anarchy, State, and Utopia*. Cambridge, MA: Harvard University Press

Urbanism lite

Joe Painter

GLOBALLY, 2007 MARKED our symbolic transition to an urban species. More than half the world's people now live in cities. Yet as we move into this mainly urban future it seems cities can no longer bear the weight of our economic, cultural and political expectations. Like an ungainly overloaded Mumbai rickshaw they are freighted with too much. They carry too many imaginings – utopian and dystopian alike. Maybe (whisper it softly) cities have had enough of Big Ideas. Just maybe we need a lighter urban sensibility that neither unfairly demonises nor naively exalts city living.

For some, cities are the bearers of salvation; for others, of damnation. We are told they will be economic powerhouses bringing competitiveness and prosperity, but also ecological calamities hastening climate change and threatening biodiversity. Cities promise security – housing, jobs, social support, and ready access to goods and services. However, they also seem increasingly vulnerable to technological failure, environmental threats and terrorist attack. They are simultaneously the cultural pinnacles of the age, enriched with architectural masterpieces, and chaotic planning disasters, bedevilled by poor design and inelegant layout. In the global south cities accrete informal settlements whose residents live in conditions that should shame us all, yet these are also 'slums of hope'.

> cities can no longer bear the weight of our expectations

Etymologically and historically cities gave us civilisation and citizenship; now they are pilloried as anti-social quagmires of incivility and hatred. The philosopher Henri Lefebvre saw the city as the leading site of social progress, but today every photographer of urban life from Manhattan to Manila juxtaposes the Lexus and the rickshaw, the penthouse and the hovel. While those iconic megacities pull on the imagination, worldwide only 15 per cent of urbanites live in cities of over 5 million inhabitants. Most live in the diverse hundreds of settlements of under a million. Can we really expect all these varied places to fulfil the gamut of our urban aspirations?

We need a lighter urbanism that does not demand from our cities more than they can give. 'Urbanism lite' will be sceptical but not cynical. It will question urban megaprojects and grand designs, but insist on the need for inspiring innovation. It will learn from Italy's 'slow cities' but will refuse to fetishise either speed or slowness. Without underestimating the importance of material prosperity for the have-nots, urbanism lite will see cities as ends and not means, as places for life and for lives, and not only for making money. It will seek the active participation of residents in planning and development, while insisting on democratic arbitration between inevitable conflicts of interest.

Graham, S. and Marvin, S. (2001) *Splintering Urbanism: Networked infrastructures, technological mobilities and the urban condition.* London: Routledge

Massey, D. (2007) *World City.* Cambridge: Polity Press

Robinson, J. (2006) *Ordinary Cities: Between modernity and development.* London: Routledge

New states, old wars: historicising Africa

Richard Reid

IN RECENT YEARS, Africa has been characterised by the emergence of national and ethnic identities rooted in violence, and this has manifested itself in both internal conflict and cross-border warfare. Nowhere is this more clearly demonstrated than in the region of northeast Africa, comprising Ethiopia, Somalia, Eritrea, Sudan and Uganda. Within this area are concentrated some of the world's most explosive zones of conflict, with escalating humanitarian crises reflecting political, economic and cultural change. Indeed there has been growing, if largely impotent, international concern over these crises: the US government perceives the region in terms of the 'war on terror', while the African Union and the UN have attempted, or are contemplating, new forms of policing and mediation.

> fragmented violence has often been a substitute for democracy

What, then, are the key issues for investigation? There is an urgent need to understand current situations on the ground, the effects of recent conflicts and political processes, and levels of popular participation and investment in prevailing political structures and processes. However, we also need to be able to historicise the current situation. Firstly, we can do this in terms of the colonial era, including patterns of hegemony, subordination and domination; the struggle for access to resources, delineation of space in terms of power and material wealth; and creation of modern borders, and thus new identities. Secondly, we need to examine the eighteenth and nineteenth centuries, with a view to understanding patterns of conflict and corridors of conflict and competition; the existence of pre-colonial frontiers and local forms of demarcation; and wars and their root causes. In other words, we need to understand modern conflicts and tensions as, firstly, stemming from more immediate events, the colonial and post-colonial era; and, secondly, as unfinished business from the pre-colonial era. But this is not simply about studying war: there is an urgent need to understand pre-colonial patterns of conflict resolution, as well as conflict instigation.

Clearly, cyclical warfare, and continual crises of legitimate authority, are fundamentally inimical to pluralistic society, popular participation, and 'democracy'. African research needs to focus on how to restore the will of the people to political discourse and process, and re-establish consent and accountability. Much modern conflict is about unfinished business: the repeated loss of sovereignty has meant the loss of right to exercise violence and 'right wrongs'; violence has, since the late eighteenth century across the region, become 'anti-state', and as it has gone underground, driven there by a series of authoritarian regimes, it has in fact become elitist in various ways, and thus inimical to popular participation. At the same time, however, violence has become desperately fragmented, and fragmented violence has often been a substitute for democracy. Yet global solutions have no place here: rather local solutions are needed for what are essentially local problems. Such research can bring together historians, geographers, anthropologists and political scientists. The way forward for the region as a whole must include a better understanding of the relationship between conflict and identity, and of the prospects for stabilisation; the answers to the questions over Africa's future more than ever lie in its deeper past.

Chabal, P. and Daloz, J.-P. (1999) *Africa Works: Disorder as political instrument.* Oxford: James Currey

Cramer, C. (2006) *Civil War Is Not a Stupid Thing: Accounting for violence in developing countries.* London: Hurst

Kaarsholm, P. (ed.) (2006) *Violence, Political Culture and Development in Africa.* Oxford: James Currey

Where in the world is the rural?

Jonathan Rigg

FOR J. H. BOEKE, working and writing in the Netherlands Indies (now Indonesia) in the 1940s, the village was a social space where notions of materialism, rationalism and individualism simply did not figure and where 'native', pre-capitalist notions of subsistence, self-reliance, community and custom controlled existence. The village community – for Boeke – was distinct from the modern city.

This stark separation of rural from urban life may no longer hold sway, even if those who study 'Development' still assume a divide between rural and urban areas, between agriculture and industry, and between peasants and workers. Embedded in these divides are a series of other powerful dissociations: between cosmopolitan urban life and living and parochial rural existences; between connection and disconnection; between marketised, commodified lives and subsistence living; and, more generally, between modernity and tradition.

> new urban classes are colonising the countryside

Development trajectories in Asia are challenging these divisions, so much so that there are questions, first, whether the categories we use continue to have much scholarly traction and, second, whether policy interventions based on the continued efficacy of such divides target the core issues.

Factories and industrial activities are colonising the countryside and the rural is becoming a space that contains – though it does not combine – both rural and urban activities, identities and processes. Villages, the elemental building blocks of the countryside, are becoming socially urban as activities, attitudes, norms of behaviour, consumption patterns, and modes of interaction become, in essence rather than in location, urban rather than rural. Households and individuals are increasingly becoming physically dislocated from their rural, natal villages. Lives are lived on the move as people oscillate between urban and rural, and field and factory. Households divided across space and sectors are replacing the co-residential dwelling unit as representative of 'normal' living. New urban classes are colonising the countryside as improving transport and communications are drawing rural areas functionally into the ambit of urban centres. Moreover, livelihoods can no longer be easily categorised, such is the degree to which occupational multiplicity has proliferated.

To illustrate the turbulence in the Asian countryside, take the case of Thailand. It is not unusual to find rural households in Thailand where land is no longer worked; where the thread of farming knowledge between the generations has been broken; where young men and women live away from home but entrust their children to their grandparents; where sons and daughters are registered as resident in one place but live in another; where villages surrounded by rice lands are supported and sustained by income from factory work; and where the buffalo is a memory. There is a deep sense that the pace and character of change in the Asian countryside is such that scholars are playing theoretical and explanatory catch-up, while governments are attempting to manage a process that they do not fully appreciate, rarely understand and, often, do not particularly like.

Boeke, J. H. (1942) *The Structure of Netherlands Indian Economy.* New York: Institute of Pacific Relations

Davis, M. (2004) 'Planet of slums: urban involution and the informal proletarian', *New Left Review* 26 (March–April): 5–34

Thompson, E. C. (2004) 'Rural villages as socially urban spaces in Malaysia', *Urban Studies* 41(12): 2357–76

The archaeology of climate change

T. J. Wilkinson

ARCHAEOLOGY HAS THE UNIQUE CAPABILITY of providing data over many thousands of years on human settlement, population trends, and impacts on the human
environment. In a world where global warming has become a
major issue, this is a significant contribution. Whereas archaeology is generally regarded as the study of ancient buildings,
cities, artefacts and ways of life, in recent years there has been
a massive growth in the study of past landscapes, settlements
and their associated environments. The data that have emerged
over the past twenty years demonstrate that following the initial
development of agriculture some 10,000 years ago, there was a
population explosion. In addition, the natural environment has
been progressively impacted as a result of biomass burning,
clearance of woodland, settlement on hill slopes, interference
with waterways and so on, all of which have contributed to the
present anthropogenic and often degraded landscape.

While the above results have been emerging from archaeology,
a parallel debate has recently appeared within the earth sciences. In 2003, William Ruddiman pointed out that the CO_2
cycle in the present interglacial was different from that of the
previous three interglacials. Specifically, Ruddiman reports
that the carbon dioxide trend started to become anomalous
and deviate from the natural cycle some 8,000 years ago. For
methane the process started some 5,000 years ago. Such trends
imply that global warming does not simply result from the
industrial revolution and modern ages, but has its origins much

earlier, namely shortly after the agricultural revolution ushered in an unprecedented phase of food production and deforestation. This model, although not entirely accepted, fits neatly with the record derived from archaeological surveys and landscape studies which demonstrate for many parts of the world that there was a significant increase in population during the early phases of sedentary occupation that accompanied the development of agriculture. Furthermore, this rapid increase in agricultural populations was compounded by the dramatic rise of cities and urban communities some 5,000 years ago. Data derived from environmental archaeology, as well as from the related fields of palaeobotany and geoarchaeology, demonstrate that loss of vegetation, destruction of organic soil horizons and soil erosion all gathered momentum over this period of time. Of course the scale of environmental degradation does not compare with that of the industrial revolution; also it is necessary to appreciate that these changes were spatially complex and temporally oscillating. Nevertheless, archaeological data point to a significant change in the pace of environmental degradation and population increase after the origins of agriculture and the start of the urban revolution, a correlation that lends credence to the Ruddiman hypothesis.

It should be emphasised that this is not another example of the denial of global warming; rather that the trajectory started considerably earlier than is normally accepted. One implication is that the biosphere and atmosphere may be more sensitive to relatively minor impacts than had been thought. Therefore, if anything, efforts to stem global warming are more urgent because of this sensitivity.

Bell, M. and Walker, M. J. C. (2005) *Late Quaternary Environmental Change, Physical and Human Perspectives*, 2nd ed. Harlow: Pearson/ Prentice Hall

Redman, C. L. (1999) *Human Impact on Ancient Environments.* Tucson, AZ: University of Arizona Press

Ruddiman, W. F. (2003) 'The anthropogenic greenhouse era began thousands of years ago', *Climatic Change* 61: 261–93

Going east

David E. Cooper

PREDICTING TOMORROW'S DEVELOPMENTS in professional philosophy is hardly an exact science. Nevertheless, there is one guess worth hazarding: there will be a growing engagement by philosophers in the West with Asian traditions of thought.

Such a rapprochement would certainly suit the mood of our times, at once respectful of 'diversity' and ecumenical in ambition. It is anyway a likely spin-off in the academic world from the emergence of China and India as mighty economic and political forces in the wider world. The signs are already there: the mushrooming of 'East-West' international conferences over the last few years; the employment in several British philosophy departments of specialists in non-Western thought; and the frequent invocation in books and articles – including ones on logic and epistemology – of ideas drawn from, say, Buddhist or Vedanta philosophy. Today, no informed American or European philosopher would concur with the judgements of Hegel and Husserl, among others, that nothing but a woolly mysticism was ever produced east of Suez.

Aesthetics is one area in particular where engagement with eastern traditions is likely to strengthen. It has been said that the vocabulary of Chinese and especially Japanese aesthetics should be the envy of any aesthetician. In such concepts as *aware* ('pathos of things'), *yūgen* (a 'mysterious' beauty intimated by the appearances of things), and *wabi-sabi* (a 'humble' beauty and patina of simple, undramatic things), we find notions of beauty and art that are sufficiently intriguing and different from any that have been central to Western thought to invite philosophical reflection and scholarly comparison with the *idées mères* of European aesthetics.

But there are wider reasons to welcome this engagement. First, the Western aesthetic attention has been almost entirely focused on the appreciation of art works (to the degree that Hegel could equate aesthetics with the philosophy of art). In the East, however, aesthetic reflection has been as much focused on the aesthetics of 'everyday life' – on tea ceremonies, for example, or the crafts – and upon the aesthetics of nature. With attention, even in the West, now turning towards the everyday, one should expect, and encourage, scholars to draw upon eastern resources. Second, there is a staleness about the questions – 'Is beauty "subjective" or "objective"?', 'What is meant by "art"?' – which have dominated Western discussions. The injection into Western aesthetic debate of issues that have always been more pressing in Japan or India – concerning, say, the relation between aesthetic and religious sensibilities, or the importance of aesthetic sensibility within the economy of a fulfilled human life – might surely invigorate a discipline whose own practitioners often lament the narrow limits within which its over-familiar programmes are pursued.

Carr, B. and Mahalingam, I. (eds.) (1996) *Companion Encyclopedia of Asian Philosophy.* Oxford: Blackwell

Odin, S. (1999) *Aesthetic Detachment in Japan and the West.* Honolulu: University of Hawai'i Press

Saito, Y. (2008) *Everyday Aesthetics.* Oxford: Oxford University Press

Why does where you are matter for how you are?

Sarah Curtis

'HEALTH' MEANS DIFFERENT THINGS to different people, but there is wide acceptance that it is more than just the 'absence of disease and infirmity'. Mental, as well as physical health is important. Increasingly, well-being is being emphasised, reminding us that there are important 'positive' dimensions to 'health', such as 'physical fitness', 'psychological resilience', 'happiness' and 'life satisfaction'. While medical care and individual lifestyle are important for health and wellbeing, the 'social model' of health is now generally accepted, showing that a wide range of conditions and processes in the wider social and physical environment are important for differences in health among individuals and social groups. Thus, how we are depends partly on where we are, combined with our individual attributes.

> health is more than the 'absence of disease'

Factors such as environmental pollution and food safety, housing quality, working conditions, school regimes and social cohesion in communities are among the many aspects of environment that contribute to our health and well-being. Many different 'settings' or 'landscapes' feature in our daily lives which may represent 'spaces of risk' for health, but may also be healing, therapeutic places that help restore or maintain good health (like spas, favourite buildings or attractive green spaces). Furthermore, especially in today's complex, globalising society, 'place' takes on new dimensions; rapid, widespread movements for work and leisure and use of internet technologies, and world-scale processes like global warming all impinge on our 'daily action space' where we routinely live, work and play. Thus health is not only determined by local conditions, but is linked in complex ways to what is happening in different parts of the world. New theories aim to conceptualise this complexity and include at least some of it in research designed to understand the 'causal pathways' linking human health and the environment.

Such knowledge needs to be interpreted and transmitted to many different actors and institutions to achieve health gains through social policy and social action. One practical approach to knowledge transfer in this field is prospective Health Impact Assessment (HIA), which involves rapid forward-looking appraisals in the early stage of formulation of new policies or plans for implementing social and economic development and building projects. The aim is to plan ahead for possible health impacts, and to learn from previous experience and research about how places can affect health. The approach to HIA is often participative, working with a range of stakeholders to consider health implications of new schemes and suggest modifications to plans in the light of knowledge about how places relate to health. This knowledge is important for efforts to improve human health and reduce health inequalities.

Curtis, S. (2004) *Health and Inequality: Geographical perspectives.* London, Sage.

Death and the web

Douglas Davies

EMOTIONS FLOW, person to person, in sympathies that foster encouragement when distressed. Historically, death was common knowledge, with the old and young encountering bereavement feelings. However, recent decades have witnessed a growing rarity of 'real death' in advanced societies as few babies die and many live long. Responsible adults seldom see a corpse until middle age and may not know how to teach the younger generation emotions of death. This unique period in cultural evolution overlaps with the advent of the World Wide Web and the daily relationship with computers that many experience, not least the young. For many of the young the maturing task of pondering life's meaning coincides with the paradoxical rarity of 'real death' and the omnipresence of 'screen-deaths' in innumerable death-games and cosmetic wonders of post-mortem cadavers in murder fiction.

> pre-screeners lived in the messy knowledge of death

As a result, death, in its www and not DNA form, becomes curious, its feelings not yet fully named as new lifestyles attract new death styles as the first mythical bite into the forbidden fruit moves to the innumerable bytes awaiting the curious. Throughout evolution, lifestyle and death style have partnered each other. Pre-screeners lived in the messy knowledge of death, in grief at the loss of children, kin and neighbour, in shared sympathy. Now, uniquely in history, lifestyle and death style diverge. Self-assured adults, never having known grief, become humanly de-skilled while their recently discovered 'emotional intelligence' identifies the gap and seeks help on-line. To 'screeners' such 'virtual' help is ever ready in myriad memorial sites for celebrities, relatives or pets; with advice on grief, but not without a shadow-side of potent lurking loneliness. For millennia, myth and doctrine fostered the epic contest of hope and death as clever brains pondered their mortality. Now www factors foster feelings of their own whose names have yet to be spoken and shared.

Intimacy and distance remain in dynamic tension as the bereaved share their feelings online with many others. The social embarrassment of grief is avoided in the intimacy of distance, which may be an adaptive advantage in societies where death is rare.

Ariès, P. (1974) *Western Attitudes Towards Death from the Middle Ages to the Present.* London: Marion Boyars

Kellehear, A. (2007) *A Social History of Dying.* Cambridge: Cambridge University Press

Seale, C. (1998) *Constructing Death.* Cambridge: Cambridge University Press

Stem cells – myths and realities

Chris J. Hutchison

THE WORDS 'STEM CELLS' conjure images of cloned embryos and almost magical cures for a wide range of diseases. As with most things that grab media attention, some of this is true and some is fiction. So what is the truth about stem cells? The really good news is that we all have stem cells and if we treat them nicely they keep us fit and healthy. Stem cells are those cells in our different organ systems that allow us to replace old or damaged cells. A good example is in skin. Every day we have to replace thousands of skin cells. This is because to make skin that is an effective barrier to our external environment, the most mature skin cells die to form a layer of fibrous material on the

> the really good news is that we all have stem cells

outer layer of our skin. This dead layer does not last long and is eventually shed and has then to be replaced by the layers of cells underneath it. Therefore there is a constant need to replace skin cells and this is achieved by stem cells.

Stem cells are different from other cells in a tissue because when they divide they are able to produce two completely different daughters. One daughter becomes another stem cell and likely goes into a state of hibernation until it is needed again (this is called self-renewal). The other daughter divides quite rapidly to generate a larger population of cells, which then take on the characteristics of the mature cells in the organ system, in this case skin (this is called differentiation). Generally this system of replacement works well but sometimes it goes wrong and when it does an individual is in danger of organ failure. This may happen when you get a disease or in response to treatment of a disease, or it may happen as a result of injury. For example, certain types of cancer such as lymphoma are treated with either chemo or radiotherapy, and the treatment not only kills your cancer cells but it also kills stem cells, particularly blood stem cells. This leads to susceptibility to infection.

Now here is the first myth and the first reality. If you listen to current media coverage you would think that stem cell therapies are new or just around the corner; but in fact stem cell therapies have been in use for over twenty years! For some time now, in treating lymphoma, physicians have sought to find a close relative, usually a sibling, who can donate his or her blood stem cells to the patient. The reason for using a sibling is that they are likely to provide a genetic match and the stem cells will therefore not be rejected, helping to repopulate the recipient's immune system.

So if stem cells are already in regular use why all the recent fuss? It is provoked by the problems that arise when you cannot be treated in this way. A child with leukaemia who has no siblings sometimes has no suitable donor. So for this child an alternative is needed and this is the idea behind embryo cloning and human Embryonic Stem Cells (hESC). Briefly, hESCs are made by taking 'spare embryos' following in vitro fertilisation. Alternatively, 'cloned embryos' can also be made for the purposes of generating hESCs. There are two main reasons for making hESCs. First, it has been surmised that these cells are genetically identical to either the embryo eventually used to produce a baby for infertile couples or the donor of the genetic material used to make a clone. This is thought to be important because the cells will not be rejected by the immune system and can be used therapeutically for individuals with the same genetic identity. This in turn is based upon the idea that however altruistic I am, I could never donate my stem cells to you because we are genetically different and your body would reject my stem cells. Secondly, hESCs are very potent and can make just about any tissue in the human body.

Here is a second myth and a new reality. In fact, I can donate some of my stem cells to you in the safe knowledge that they will not be rejected. Colin Jahoda of Durham University performed a remarkable experiment some years ago proving this point. He discovered a population of stem cells that reside under the skin, and organise other skin cells to make hair. These cells have some extraordinary properties. Jahoda found that he could transplant these cells into the forearm of another unrelated person and they would make hairs grow by organising the hair-making capacity of surrounding cells. This was remarkable for two reasons: first, the stem cells did what they were supposed to do in another person, and, secondly, they were not rejected. Later, in collaboration with another close colleague, Nick Hole, he was able to show that these same stem cells that normally helped to form hair could, if injected into bone marrow, make blood!

The significant point is that Jahoda had discovered a source of stem cells that could be isolated very easily and which had potentially wide therapeutic uses, so perhaps avoiding the need for spare or cloned embryos to make hESCs. This is not to condemn cloning; indeed every avenue should be explored to fight disease. However, it appears that therapies of the power that we are currently reading about are perhaps closer than we had previously imagined and may not require the use of techniques which some people find ethically questionable.

Lako, M., Armstrong, L., Cairns, P. M., Harris, S., Hole, N. and Jahoda, C. A. B. (2002) 'Hair follicle dermal cells repopulate the mouse haematopoietic system', *Journal of Cell Science* 115(20): 3967–74

Reynolds, A. J., Lawrence, C., Cserhalmi-Friedman, P. B., Christiano, A. M. and Jahoda, C. A. B. (1999) 'Trans-gender induction of hair follicles', *Nature* (402): 33–34

Creativity and health

Jane Macnaughton

THE FIRST EXHIBITION HALL you enter at the Melbourne Immigration Museum tells the stories in words and pictures of those who have left their home countries to settle in Australia. The accounts are grouped under a number of themes, including 'war', 'famine', 'natural disasters' and 'the search for a better life'. In the final section, a young Indian man's voice accompanies film of groups of people crowding round a pier: 'I needed to leave my country to fulfil the potential I knew was inside me'. After the scenes of desolation and waste of human life these images and his voice vividly capture the clamouring need for human beings not just to survive and live, but to live well. Indeed this young man expressed a higher need, that is for us to live a flourishing life that makes use of the innate talents and potential within us. One important prerequisite for the flourishing human life is good health, and in terms of health status, migration from a developing to a developed country seems like a good move. In the West we now experience better health and longevity than ever before, but it appears that we do not *enjoy* it. As Roy Porter eloquently puts it: 'These are strange times when we are healthier than ever but more anxious about our health'.

> an important prerequisite for flourishing life is good health

This is a complex problem and in thinking about issues of health and well-being we must acknowledge the importance of collective and integrated insights from the many disciplines trained upon it. For most of us, questions of health concern medicine, and medicine is seen as primarily a scientific discipline employing a rigorous evidence-based approach to dealing with illness and its treatment. However, questions of health, illness and disease are also, for all of us, questions about what we *experience* in our daily lives, rather than how a textbook or study tells us it should be. When we go to the doctor, we seek help for experiential problems – concerning how we as individuals feel or what we are able to do. Moreover, an important source of information about individual human experience is the humanities, especially literature, but also art, history, classics, theology and philosophy.

In the Anglo-American context this 'medical humanities' approach to health has tended to focus on the revitalisation of medical education, recognising that medical students need rebalancing towards a greater understanding of individual patient experience. We have offered students this through specific literary readings, films and discussions. This approach has its place in the bigger question of the 'flourishing life' as those students who actually engage with this literary approach have commented on how literature brings alive medical studies which can seem initially distanced from the job of patient care. However, we are now seeking to investigate how the use of arts and humanities can potentiate experience not just of medical education but also of health care and health itself.

Work with schools, hospitals, wider community organisations and medical students – with individuals responsible for delivering health care and those in receipt of it – has suggested that the ground rock of scientific understanding on which health-care delivery is based needs to be tempered with a greater understanding of how individuals actually experience their lives. In particular, we suspect that involvement in creativity either as a participant or a viewer is in some way essential to human flourishing. More work is needed to tease out the details of this complex association and an interdisciplinary approach linking humanities, science and social science will further investigate the questions that much empirical work continues to raise.

Marmot, M. (2004) *Status Syndrome: How your social standing directly affects your health and life expectancy.* London: Bloomsbury

Porter R. (1997) *The Greatest Benefit to Mankind: A medical history of humanity from antiquity to the present.* London: HarperCollins

Wilson, M. (1975) *Health Is for People.* London: Longman

Making a purse out of a sow's ear

Paul Yeo

THE IMPACT THAT VIRUSES have on human health cannot be underestimated. But something beneficial can be made from viruses; indeed, the very aspects that make them scary can be manipulated in the laboratory to help us in our fight against disease.

For many years now particular viruses have been used as vehicles in gene therapy. We have learnt how to manipulate their genomes, insert a human gene and use these hybrid viruses to infect patients suffering from a debilitating illness. The most significant of these interventions lies in the fight against cystic fibrosis (CF), a chronic lung disease caused by a defect in a single protein expressed on the surface of cells. A virus carrying a gene encoding a 'normal' copy of the defective protein is used to infect patients in order to correct the disorder. But these viruses can infect cells other than those that they are used to target. Indeed, the CF story is a case in point. Recent clinical trials, whilst successful in tackling CF, were halted as patients developed hepatic cancer.

something beneficial can be made from viruses

Therefore we need to improve the safety of interventions. One idea is to develop viruses that infect specific cells, and we are now establishing a greater understanding of how to do this. All viruses have an attachment protein, a protein that allows a virus to grab onto a cell. Some of these attachment proteins do not appear to have any cell type specificity, but some do. A good

130

example is HIV. Its attachment protein, gp120, binds to a molecule called CD4 found mainly on a subset of T cells, cells that are important in regulating our immune system; hence HIV kills these cells, the ability to fight off infection is lost as a result, and patients succumb to AIDS. But if we can manipulate the virus-receptor interaction we may be able to target viruses to cells that we wish to infect. One of the first attempts to do this was with Foot and Mouth Disease Virus (FMDV), in order to make it safer to work with in the pursuit of a vaccine. The FMDV was genetically modified, changing its receptor affinity so that the virus would only recognise a cell line expressing a specific foreign protein rather than the native viral receptor. In this way the virus produced could not infect normal cells and would not represent a threat if accidentally released. To take this idea one step further we can then think of changing a viral receptor protein so that it recognises a unique protein found on only one or on a limited number of cell types.

Therefore by manipulating viral attachment proteins we can induce infection of specific cells, thus targeting our gene therapy delivery vehicles to where they are needed. But we need to improve our knowledge of what is expressed on what cell types in order to develop a repertoire of specific targets.

Waehler, R., Russell, S. J. and Curiel, D. T. (2007) 'Engineering targeted viral vectors for gene therapy', *Nat Rev Genet* 8: 573–87

Wiznerowicz, M. and Trono, D. (2005) 'Harnessing HIV for therapy, basic research and biotechnology', *Trends Biotechnol* 23: 42–7

Building with light

Colin Bain

THREE HUNDRED YEARS have elapsed since Newton's *Opticks* provided a firm scientific basis for the study of light, and more than a century has passed since Einstein's theory of special relativity established the central role of the speed of light in modern physics. Yet light still remains at the heart of research in the physical sciences and retains its ability to surprise. In the 1990s, the public imagination was captured by photonic crystals – materials with regular arrays of cavities (similar to the natural mineral, opal) in which only certain colours of light are able to exist. The first decade of this century has seen the emergence of metamaterials: substances that can bend light round an object in such a way that to the external observer it appears that the object is not there. While there is undoubtedly fascinating physics in metamaterials, the public impact has been greatly magnified by allusions to Harry Potter's invisibility cloak! On the astronomical length scale, the ever-so-small variations in the cosmic background of microwaves provide one of the few direct windows onto the processes occurring at the birth of our universe. At the other extreme of the length scale, fluorescence imaging can track single biological molecules in cells with nanometre (a millionth of a millimetre) precision.

> light still retains its ability to surprise

Light has long been used to pattern surfaces. The whole of the microelectronics industry relies on the illumination through masks of light-sensitive polymers called photoresists, which can subsequently be etched away to reveal intricate patterns on the semiconductors below. In 2001, in a beautiful demonstration of microfabrication with photoresists, Dr Kawata from Osaka University fashioned a Japanese bull so small that ten thousand bulls could fit on a pin-head. Light can also be used directly to shape and assemble matter on a microscopic length scale. With the acceptance of wave-particle duality at the beginning of the twentieth century came the realisation that small 'particles' of light – photons – carry momentum and therefore can exert forces on objects that they strike. It was not until the invention of optical tweezers by Ashkin at Bell labs in 1986, however, that it became practical to use light as a mechanical tool. In optical tweezers, a laser beam is passed through a high-magnification objective lens. Small particles, typically from 0.1 to 10 microns across (a micron is a thousandth of a millimetre), are trapped at the focus of the laser beam and can then be picked up and moved around. Large numbers of such traps can be implemented simultaneously and used to arrange particles in predefined patterns in two or three dimensions. More remarkably, micron-sized particles that are uniformly illuminated by a laser beam can spontaneously assemble into regular arrays. The only force holding the wall together is the light scattered from one sphere to another: turn off the laser beam and the array disintegrates in the blink of an eye. Replace the solid spheres by liquid droplets of oil in water and light becomes a sculptor's tool, pulling and shaping the droplet into dumbbells, triangles or squares. The ability of light to assemble and shape matter on a microscopic scale presents an exciting playground that we are only just beginning to explore.

Grier, D. (2003) 'A Revolution in Optical Manipulation', *Nature* 424: 810

Mullins, J. (2006) 'The Stuff of Beams: Building with light', *New Scientist* 2551: 44

Sanderson, K. (2007) 'Materials Science: Unexpected tricks of light', *Nature* 446: 364

Seeing by looking

John Findlay

HOW DO WE SEE? Vision is the primary human sense; it involves as much as half of the brain. Yet we still have no accepted and comprehensive theory of how we see. We know

that the eye forms an image on the retina,

the brain's operations are fundamentally predictive

which is encoded in a set of neural impulses that are passed to the brain along about one million fibres of the optic nerve. The most popular approach to under-standing vision has been to concentrate on what then happens within the brain, with its enormous computational potential.

However, this approach has encountered problems, for while it says something about seeing, it entirely ignores looking. Focusing on looking leads to a new perspective, for example by helping us to understand how the eye conducts search.

As well as being designed for seeing, our eyes are exquisitely well designed for looking. Each eye can be rotated by six powerful muscles and during everyday vision these muscles are hard at work. The eyes rest in one position for a fraction of a second and then a new position is selected. Another feature of the eye only makes sense when looking is taken into account. We possess an amazing capacity for resolution of visual detail but this acute vision is greatest only in a very small region, the fovea, and declines systematically outside this region. It is necessary to direct the gaze to important locations in order to see effectively.

The process of seeing by looking, termed active vision, has led to a new and crucial set of questions about vision. How is the decision made that the eyes should move? How do the eyes choose where to look next? How can we be so unaware that our retinal images are continually changing?

One area of investigation where the active vision perspective has long proved fruitful is the process of reading printed and written text. Here it has been demonstrated that the amount taken in at each eye pause is relatively small, but nonetheless it is taken in an anticipatory way, concentrating on the location where the gaze will land next, as well as the one where the gaze currently rests. This illustrates a general feature of brain activity that is being increasingly recognised: the brain's operations are fundamentally predictive.

Work in visual search has shown another important way that the brain operates. If a previously encountered search display is seen again, the search process operates more quickly even though the searcher has no ability at all to recognise that the display has been seen before. Implicit memory processes, which may be called tacit knowledge, are increasingly recognised as playing an important role in the control of behaviour.

Findlay, J. M. and Gilchrist, I. D. (2003) *Active Vision: The psychology of looking and seeing.* Oxford: Oxford University Press

Hayhoe, M. and Ballard, D. (2005) 'Eye movements in natural behaviour', *Trends in Cognitive Sciences* 9: 188–94

Liversedge, S. P. and Findlay, J. M. (2000) 'Saccadic eye movements and cognitive science', *Trends in Cognitive Sciences* 4: 6–14

Reflections on light

Giles Gasper

THE VARIETY OF WAYS in which light has been conceived and described gives it a central place in the human experience. As a theme for study, light is potentially all-encompassing. It holds a central significance for the way in which the physical world is interpreted, affects fundamentally the way in which the built environment is conceived, acts as a powerful literary image and poetic metaphor, and plays an important role in religious reflection.

The understanding and use of light is of particular interest in the field of medieval intellectual history, where the role played and position taken by light cannot be underestimated. Within the Judaeo-Christian tradition, light is crucial to the story of creation – light is created on the first day in the first Biblical account in Genesis 1, and provides a constant image of God, Christ and salvation. The intellectual challenge for western Christendom of the twelfth and thirteenth centuries was the absorption of Aristotelian (and to a more limited extent Platonic) learning into a Christian framework. How light was explained and discussed, both in terms of the genesis of creation and as a physical phenomenon, was vital to this exercise of absorption.

> texts on light reveal much about the transmission of new learning

The attempt to re-create the action of rainbows led to some of the first experiments in the western scientific tradition in the thirteenth century. On a more metaphysical front, the imagery of light suffused the growing mystical literature of this period. Reflection on the mystical qualities of light took physical as well as literary form, notably in the emergence of Gothic architecture, but also in a host of other material arts, from jewellery cutting to metalwork. Secular authors too used light as an image; the play of light on the weaponry of assembled armies a common theme. In the *Paradiso*, Dante develops a multi-faceted language of light to depict with almost scientific precision his imaginings of heaven.

Study of the understanding and use of light unlocks, potentially, a diverse number of themes within the study of the Middle Ages, its religious, spiritual and mystical outlooks, its conceptions of the physical world and universe and its artistic and aesthetic values. Texts on light reveal much about the transmission of new learning within medieval Europe, but also, especially through Spain, Sicily and Constantinople, between Latin Christendom and its neighbouring civilisations. The theme of light also allows for extended reflection on the way in which medieval attitudes towards the authoritative texts of the past – classical, biblical and patristic – were formulated and changed. The understanding of light is a theme that lies at the very heart of intellectual and cultural changes within a period central to the development of western scientific, theological and philosophical thought.

Armstrong, A. H. (ed.) (1967) *The Cambridge History of Later Greek and Early Medieval Philosophy.* Cambridge: Cambridge University Press

McEvoy, J. (1982) *The Philosophy of Robert Grosseteste.* Oxford: Oxford University Press

Scanning your future

David Parker

OVER NINETY YEARS AGO, the Italian poet Ungaretti reflected upon the image of the sea and sky: 'M'illumino d'immenso'. This phrase equally might define our thinking about what we could and should be able to do, over the next century, by capturing new accurate images of the human body.

We strive to develop non-invasive methods that can give reliable information about the health or disease state of our bodies. We do this because we want to know if our health is compromised by the onset of disease or malignancy. At present, we rely upon various diagnostic tests or scans to help us assess this. Often, the scan is only taken if the diagnostic test suggests it is needed. Sadly, many current 'tests' and scans are just not good enough. In male prostate cancer screening, 70 per cent of the PSA (prostate specific antigen) tests are false-positives; in breast screening 75 per cent of mammograms give false positives – this is a huge waste of effort and places undue stress on millions of patients. If we can spend huge sums of money scanning for items in our baggage at airports, surely we can develop sophisticated scanning methods that will highlight arterial narrowing or the genesis of a malignancy?

Most scans rely upon the interaction of electromagnetic radiation with tissue or bone, but the instrumentation is very expensive, time available is limited and their distribution favours large clinical centres. Well known to most of us are the X-ray scan and the MRI scan. The X-ray scan is used to examine skeletal features, most usefully in dental practice and in breast/lung cancer screening. Since the late 1980s, more and more clinical centres are now able to offer images based on the analysis of the distribution of water in the human body, commonly known as an MRI scan. It is certainly true that MRI is a superior technique to X-ray tomography and should replace many X-ray methods, in time, once the instrumentation becomes cheaper. How useful it would be, for example, if we could assess the progression of arthritis in our GP medical centre, simply by putting our hand into a portable imager to reveal the extent of inflammation. But we should not be content simply to define anatomical features with 100-micron resolution, we need to find ways that would allow the key markers of early disease to be signalled and quantified. These markers may be traced to the action of one chemical or set of chemicals or another. So we need to find new and simpler imaging modalities or modifications of current methods, that encode spatial and temporal information

we need superior and cheaper clinical imaging methods

at the molecular level, that can, for example, signal the onset of the 207 different forms of cancer or that can indicate the onset of arterial narrowing and atherosclerosis (stroke/ischaemia/coronary heart disease).

How are we to address these problems? First, we require more accurate diagnostic tests or sensors, linked to responsive imaging protocols. Good and reliable methods now assess the onset of pregnancy or the status of diabetic hyperglycaemia. We need similar quick, cheap and portable tests or sensors that can examine various readily available bio-fluids (saliva/urine, seminal fluid) and allow the onset of renal disease, liver decay or prostate cancer to be signalled confidently. Coupled with this we need superior and cheaper, more portable, clinical imaging methods that can allow the progression of disease to be assessed accurately or the response to therapy measured.

This will require the development of new imaging modalities – photoacoustic imaging, for example – or the introduction of methods (e.g. chemical shift imaging in magnetic resonance) that allow changes in the concentration of key reporter metabolites to be quantified, in real time and with high spatial resolution. They can then be used to guide therapy.

Only then might we be 'enlightened by the immensity' of our achievement.

Parker, D., Pandya, S. and Yu, J. (2006) 'Engineering emissive lanthanide complexes for molecular imaging and sensing', *Dalton Trans.* 2757–66

Weissleder, R. (2006) 'Molecular imaging in cancer', *Science* 312: 1168–71

Eye-aye

Roy Quinlan

IT IS THE EYE that has provided medicine with some of the most important breakthroughs over the past century. The accessibility of the eye and the impact that sight-depriving diseases have on people has meant that ophthalmology has often led medicine in some of its most exciting advances. The development of tissue transplantation (cornea), non-invasive surgical techniques (laser technologies), novel anti-viral treatments (retinoblastoma), gene replacement (retina) and stem cell therapies (cornea), tissue engineering and functional prostheses (cornea/retina/lens) were all led by research into the eye, and the eye is not ready to give up centre-stage just yet; the next arena will be a 'new for old' policy for ageing tissues. Why should the eye hold such influence? The most common neurodegenerative disease is not Huntington's or Parkinson's Disease or even Alzheimer's Disease, but Age Related Macular Degeneration (AMD), a condition that affects the neurons in the retina. The most common cause of sight deprivation in the UK, however, is not AMD, but cataract – a staggering 250,000 new NHS cases every year. Both diseases are set to rise dramatically over the next few decades as the life expectancy of our population increases. Now, of course, innovative therapies are needed for their treatment.

> the most common cause of sight deprivation in the UK is cataract

Failing eyesight is also one of the most powerful arguments to sway public opinion on the importance of eye research because everyone experiences this as they get older. The evidence of our advancing years is in 'our face' so to speak – it is called presbyopia. Which one of us over the age of fifty does not have varifocal/bifocal solutions to this most obvious of ageing phenomena? What would you give to have a new set of eyes to last another fifty years? A solution to presbyopia could potentially come from updating our current treatment for cataract, based on an invention by Sir Harold Ridley in 1949. We have now discovered that the eye lens, like the liver, has the power to regenerate itself and the first experiments have now been completed to show that the optical properties of a re-grown lens are superior to any man-made solution – at least for the first patient, a rabbit! New research has identified the growth factor and three-dimensional cues of the lens capsule that are required for lens cell proliferation and differentiation. The proteins that determine the optical properties of the eye lens are now known. With this knowledge base, a bioengineering solution to presbyopia and cataract using lens regeneration is possible. Optical-based technologies could offer more immediate aid to AMD sufferers (Love, Myers and Smithson; Departments of Physics and Pyschology) and assist in the detection of diabetic retinopathy (Holliman, Department of Computer Science) in partnership with clinical collaborators. Both are being developed in Durham, as are new therapies for future corneal prostheses and transplantation. This 'eye-opening' interdisciplinary research epitomises the translational environment at Durham, which is striving to make a difference to the health and well-being of our society.

Revolutionary therapies for twenty-first-century medicine – the eyes have it … again!!

Gwon, A. (2006) 'Lens regeneration in mammals: a review', *Surv Ophthalmol* 51: 51–62

Sandilands, A., Prescott, A. R., Wegener, A., Zoltoski, R. K., Hutcheson, A. M., Masaki, S., Kuszak, J. R. and Quinlan, R. A. (2003) 'Knockout of the intermediate filament protein CP49 destabilises the lens fibre cell cytoskeleton and decreases lens optical quality, but does not induce cataract', *Exp Eye Res* 76: 385–91

Tholozan, F. M., Gribbon, C., Li, Z., Goldberg, M. W., Prescott, A. R., McKie, N. and Quinlan, R. A. (2007) 'FGF-2 release from the lens capsule by MMP-2 maintains lens epithelial cell viability', *Mol Biol Cell* 18: 4222–31

Twinkle, Twinkle, Little Star

Ray Sharples

LIGHT POLLUTION is one of the most rapidly growing threats to our environment. The resultant increase of the brightness of the night sky is not only damaging our view of the starry sky but is altering our perception of dark and moonlit nights and even our physical and mental health. It is only recently that these effects of outdoor lighting have been recognised. Light pollution also indicates wasted energy, since upward-directed light does not usually provide useful or intended illumination. Dealing with light pollution and its adverse effects is a complex issue, with potential conflicts of interest between the utility providers, environmentalists, astronomers, the lighting industry and various government agencies.

> light pollution alters even our physical and mental health

Satellite images looking down at the Earth at night have been available since the early 1970s. They measure the light beamed upwards from sources on the Earth's surface but do not give any direct information about the effects of this light pollution on the night sky brightness, as observed by humans on the surface of the Earth, or about its impact on the visibility of stars. These effects may be calculated by including a physical model of the effects of scattering of light by air molecules and other small particles. Maps that show this calculated sky brightness have now been prepared for the entire world and provide a vivid record of the growth of light pollution in both developed urban areas and less densely populated areas. Assuming average eye sensitivity, about one fifth of the world's population, more than two thirds of the US population and more than one half of the EU population are estimated to have already lost naked eye visibility of the Milky Way. The only place on continental Europe where the night sky retains its natural darkness is in northern Scandinavia.

Since the early 1980s, a global dark-sky movement has been emerging, led by astronomers wishing to protect their scientific environment, but now extending to concerned people from a variety of backgrounds campaigning to reduce the amount of light pollution and improve mankind's view of the heavens. This includes the introduction of lighting legislation which aims to reduce the excessive use of light, and to encourage the use of *full cutoff* lighting fixtures which minimise the chance for light to escape above the horizontal plane where it can contribute to the sky glow. Unless this is brought under control soon, by the middle of this century children living in urban areas may never know the answer to the question 'Daddy, what does a star look like?' It is up to all of us to ensure that this does not happen.

Cinzano, P., Falchi, F., Elvidge, C. D. (2001) 'The First World Atlas of the Artificial Night Sky Brightness', *Mon. Not. Royal Astron. Soc.* 328: 689

Cinzano, P. (ed) (2000) 'Measuring and Modelling Light Pollution', *Mem. Soc. Astron. It.* 71

Rich, C. and Longcore, T. (eds.) (2005) *Ecological Consequences of Artificial Night Lighting.* Washington: Island Press

History as the story of ordinary people

Julian Wright

HISTORIANS OF EARLIER GENERATIONS have often analysed the leaders of society, the politicians and the thinkers. Old-fashioned histories of the 'great man' were described as remote from the experience of 'real people'. But the answer to the problem was not found by those social historians who were, in the 1960s, in the vanguard of a new approach to history. Replacing big men with the giant struggles of classes and economies did not in itself bring ordinary people to the fore. More recently, post-modernism has provided another trap. It rightly encouraged historians to consider the texts through which the past is transmitted to us; but sometimes this new sensitivity to the text became an obsession in itself, detracting from the real people we hope to encounter through texts.

> historians need to place the little people at the centre

By giving greater weight to individual experience, unexpected layers of complexity have been uncovered. Long-standing historical problems are being revealed by modern historians in quite new ways. Historians concerned with Germany and Russia in the 1930s, for example, increasingly use individual life-stories to understand this tortuous period. The choices of ordinary people can be more complex than those of the great. It can be harder to explain the decisions of middle-ranking civil servants in the Nazi bureaucracy than those of Hitler himself. Minor figures are less accountable for their private views, and their motivations may often be more contingent and unpredictable. Thus history is now reaching out not only to biography, but to other associated areas: family life, the processes of growing up and growing old, and the interaction of humans and their immediate environment, in the home, the club, the workplace or the holiday camp. This highly focused work feeds back into larger historical syntheses, refreshing and sometimes overturning long-held views of historical change.

After a century in which little people suffered in the name of 'great' ideas or systems, historians badly need to discover better ways of placing the little people at the centre of our analysis. If, in so doing, historians have to relinquish the claim that we can seek to explain the past through sweeping systems or formulae, then so much the better. It is no paradox to say that, by focusing on the stories told by the 'little' people, historians may in fact come closer to realising their one big, motivating idea: the notion that we have a duty to rediscover and represent human existence in all its complexity.

Harris, R. (1999) *Lourdes: Body and Spirit in the Secular Age*. London: Allen Lane

Hellbeck, J. (2006) *Revolution on My Mind: Writing a diary under Stalin*. Cambridge, MA: Harvard University Press

Schmidt, U. (2007) *Karl Brandt – the Nazi Doctor: Medicine and power in the Third Reich*. London: Hambledon

The dual nature of thought

Aidan Feeney and David Over

HOW DO WE THINK? How do we choose what shirt to put on in the morning, which horse to back in the Grand National, whether we would have done better at school had we worked harder, or what follows from a conditional statement such as 'if the light on the right is flashing then the reactor is overheating'? To answer these questions many research-ers in reasoning, decision-making and judgement are turning to the idea that there are two types of thinking. Type 1 thought is evolutionarily old, associative, fast, parallel and driven by knowledge and context. Type 2 thought is evolutionarily more recent, rule-based, slow, sequential, and is necessary for us to think about the abstract and logical structure of problems and decisions, independent of their particular content and context.

> how do we choose which horse to back in the Grand National?

One great advantage of such dualist thinking is that it allows researchers interested in different aspects of thinking to inte-grate their perspectives. Nowhere can this be seen more clearly than in recent work on the relationship between conditional reasoning and decision-making. Neither scientific nor ordinary discourse can do without conditionals. Consider an example: 'If global warming continues then London will be flooded.' It is possible that we would reason about this example using Type 2 processes, thinking about its logical structure, independent of our beliefs about global warming and its relation to flooding. Until very recently, psychological approaches assumed that people's reasoning was rule-based and sequential, failing to capture adequately the roles of content and context, which affect people's probability judgements.

But there is now much evidence that people's understanding of an ordinary conditional, 'London will be flooded, if global warming continues,' is determined by their probability judgements, which can be Type 1. For example, people may have a low-level Type 1 belief that flooding is likely under the supposition that global warming will continue. This work implies that people's understanding of conditionals depends at least as much on their Type 1 processes as on their higher-level Type 2 logical processes. Conditional reasoning can be related to decision-making because both are the joint result of Type 1 processes that are sensitive to beliefs and Type 2 processes that are sensitive to logical structure. This insight will enable us to understand human reasoning and decision-making much more deeply, with valuable consequences for artificial intelligent systems that will much more closely represent human reasoning and decision-making.

Bennett, J. (2003) *A Philosophical Guide to Conditionals.* Oxford: Oxford University Press

Evans, J. St. B. T. and Over, D. E. (2004) *If.* Oxford: Oxford University Press

Sloman, S. (1996) 'The empirical case for two systems of reasoning', *Psychological Bulletin* 119: 3–22

Voices of the mind

Charles Fernyhough

THE IDEA THAT LANGUAGE has a part to play in thinking goes back to the earliest civilisations. Plato, for example, characterised thinking as an internal dialogue, in which one is constantly answering questions posed to the self. In modern times, the greatest contribution to our understanding of how language shapes cognition came from L. S. Vygotsky. Vygotsky's starting point was that our thinking is inherently social. Interactions which initially unfold between people (say, a parent and child engaged in solving a jigsaw puzzle) become progressively internalised over the course of development to form individual verbal thought or inner speech. Two important implications flow from this idea: first, that thinking (like human social interaction) is mediated by language, and, secondly, that the thinking processes that result retain the dialogic structure of the social interactions from which they develop. Plato's 'dialogue with the self' arises, therefore, through the gradual internalisation of the dialogues we enter into with others from the earliest days of life.

> private speech can be measured through watching children solve simple puzzles

This developmental process of the internalisation of dialogue proceeds in stages. For example, as children gradually master the use of language for regulating their own thinking and behaviour, they pass through a transitional stage during which they speak their thoughts aloud. This self-directed talk is known as private speech, and it can be measured through observations of children solving simple puzzles. Children who use more of this kind of speech seem to see a benefit for their problem-solving behaviour. We have found evidence that this shift towards verbal mediation is important in other domains of thinking as well. One challenge for the future is to determine how developmental language problems, such as are associated with autism or Specific Language Impairment, affect children's ability to mediate their thinking through words. Another is to work out whether the observed associations between the so-called executive functions (those aspects of thinking relating to planning, inhibition and control) and children's social understanding may be due to the fact that both domains of cognition are mediated by language.

This view of how words 'get into the head' has implications far beyond the study of child development. We have started to apply Vygotskian ideas to understanding disorders of consciousness such as auditory verbal hallucinations, commonly associated with psychiatric disorders like schizophrenia. It may be that, in certain circumstances, the voices that make up our ordinary dialogic inner speech become mistakenly attributed to an external source, leading to the experience of a hallucination. Cognitive scientists are also increasingly interested in how internalised language can 'knit together' aspects of brain function that might otherwise remain separate. Perhaps the greatest challenge of all is to understand how this developmental process affects the changing organisation of the developing brain. Today's developmental cognitive neuro-scientists are exploring how the experience of linguistically mediated social interaction can alter the functional organisation of the brain itself, with brain and society 'co-constructing' each other. Words may not, therefore, just be a useful tool of thought; they may play a role in rewiring our brains to alter the kinds of thinking we can do.

Carruthers, P. (2002) 'The cognitive functions of language', *Behavioral and Brain Sciences 25:* 657–726

Luria, A. R. (1965) 'L. S. Vygotsky and the problem of localization of functions', *Neuropsychologia 3:* 387–92

Vygotsky, L. S. (1987) (1934) *Thinking and Speech.* In *The Collected Works of L. S. Vygotsky,* Vol. 1. New York: Plenum

Models and reality

Michael Goldstein

A 2005 *GUARDIAN* LEADER contained the following:

> The weight of evidence makes it clear that climate change is
> a real and present danger ... the chances of the Gulf stream
> – the Atlantic thermohaline circulation that keeps Britain
> warm – shutting down are now thought to be greater than
> 50%.

How was this conclusion reached? What can we learn about
reality from necessarily imperfect computer simulators?

Consider, for example, the leading climate model at the UK
Met Office. It has (at least) a hundred uncertain parameters,
expressing the effect of clouds, convection, sea ice, radiation
and boundary layer effects. And yet a few hundred evaluations
of the model are the main resource for UK Climate Impacts
Programme 2008, the definitive statement about how climate
change will impact the UK.

So, consider further the uncertainties involved in this project.
First, we don't know the appropriate values for the model
parameters. Secondly, we can only observe a tiny fraction of the
possible evaluations of the climate simulator. Thirdly, even if
evaluated at the appropriate input values, the simulator output
would not be equal to true future climate. Finally, although we
may calibrate the model to historical observations, such data
always has measurement error.

Currently, there is no satisfactory and accepted methodology for coherently dealing with all of these uncertainties. However, this area is the focus of much interest and powerful new methodology is being developed to address these issues. This methodology is based upon the Bayesian approach to statistics, which combines expert judgements with observational data, to create probability judgements that the expert should make, given initial knowledge and observations.

The necessary technology is in its early days. However, much progress is being made. For example, work at Durham started with oil reservoir simulators, which are high-dimensional and slow to evaluate. We synthesised expert elicitation, historical data and simulator evaluations to carry out essential tasks such as history matching; identifying 'correct' simulator settings.

Our approach is implemented in oil industry software. Here is an example of the software performance as reported to us. The problem was to match an oil field containing 650 wells, based on 1 million grid cells, for each of which permeability, porosity, fault lines, etc. were unknown inputs. Finding the previous best match took one man-year of effort. Our Bayesian approach, from scratch, found a match using 32 runs, automatically chosen by the software, with a fourfold improvement according to the oil company measure of match quality.

the UK Met Office has (at least) a hundred uncertain parameters

All modellers, irrespective of their discipline, are aware of the potential problems involved in using their models to address real-world problems. It is a reasonable hope that this reality gap will soon become smaller and far more transparent, with enormous practical consequences.

Goldstein, M. and Rougier, J. C. (2005) 'Probabilistic formulations for transferring inferences from mathematical models to physical systems', *SIAM Journal on Scientific Computing*, 26: 467–87

O'Hagan, A. (2006) 'Bayesian analysis of computer code outputs: a tutorial', *Reliability Engineering and System Safety*, 91: 1290–1300

Santner, T., Williams, B. and Notz, W. (2003) *The Design and Analysis of Computer Experiments*. New York: Springer Verlag

Unity of mind

Wolfram Hinzen

CONTEMPORARY DEVELOPMENTAL and comparative psychology challenges traditional presuppositions about what 'thoughts' non-linguistic animals can think. As evolution crafts minds, it does not necessarily craft channels of externalisation: mental life may be rich, but a language to get it into the open may be a step that only one species has managed to take.

This confronts us with a fundamental ethical problem. A robust notion of 'non-linguistic thought' is needed if we are to live up to the obligations that we have towards beings with a mind. We are so accustomed to specify what a language-less autistic child, a pre-linguistic baby, a chimpanzee, or an aphasic 'cannot do', that we forget

> a basic unity of mind pervades the human race

how little the lack of a shared medium of communication implies for what mind may be there, and hence for what demands our respect. Just as Descartes's view, that language-less beings are automata, has normative consequences (we can treat them in whatever way we like), the insight that they are not has such consequences as well.

A basic unity of mind pervades the human race and claims about fundamental differences in mental organisation induced by linguistic difference have by now been put to rest. All human languages share a core of computational mechanisms rooted in the architecture of the brain that do not exhibit any relevant biological difference. Human language does not co-vary with human culture, and the degree of industrialisation of a culture implies virtually nothing for the complexity of its language. Does this basic mind-plan extend to our moral faculty? Could moral systems across the globe ultimately be variations on a common theme in the way that human grammars are? What are the ethical imperatives that would ensue? The answers can only be found in language, but they bear on the realm where no language reigns.

Hauser, M. D., Chomsky, N., Fitch, W. T. (2002) 'The faculty of language: what is it, who has it, and how did it evolve?', *Science* 298: 1569–79

Hinzen, W. (2006) *Mind Design and Minimal Syntax.* Oxford: Oxford University Press

Existential feelings

Matthew Ratcliffe

IN RECENT YEARS, there has been a resurgence of scientific and philosophical interest in emotion and feeling. For the most part, discussion has been restricted to 'standard' emotions, such as anger, fear, joy, jealousy, happiness and so forth. Many of the feelings that we relate to each other in our everyday lives do not appear on such lists. Amongst those that do not are a group of feelings that we might call 'existential feelings', those feelings which constitute a background sense of reality, meaningfulness and belonging. For example, there are

> all experience incorporates a background feeling of belonging to a world

feelings of unreality, heightened existence, surreality, familiarity, unfamiliarity, deadness, emptiness, significance, insignificance, belonging, being at home in the world, being at one with things, being alive, and the list goes on.

Changes in existential feeling are especially pronounced in illnesses such as depression and schizophrenia. Psychiatric patients often complain that everything feels strangely unfamiliar, unreal or uncanny, that experience as a whole is characterised by an unbearable feeling of isolation and estrangement or that all purpose and meaning has gone from experience. These predicaments seem to be extreme manifestations of existential feelings that also occur in everyday life. Such feelings have received insufficient attention to date, partly because they do not fit into established categories of affective state, such as 'mood' and 'emotion', and partly because it is just not clear what they are.

So, what are existential feelings and in what sense are they 'feelings'? They cannot be 'bodily feelings', if we adopt the usual assumption that a bodily feeling is just an awareness of the body or part of the body. However, orthodox conceptions of bodily feeling can be challenged by drawing on the insights of philosophers working in the phenomenological tradition. As Merleau-Ponty (1962) appreciates, the feeling body is not just an object of perception but also a means by which we perceive the world. Many kinds of bodily feeling are not feelings of one's own bodily state but ways of relating to the world that shape how both the body and the surrounding world are experienced. For example, an uncomfortable feeling of overall bodily conspicuousness can at the same time be an all-encompassing sense of detachment from the world.

We can draw on phenomenology to support the view that certain feelings constitute a general sense of belonging to a world and of the world's reality, rather than ways in which more specific objects, events or situations are experienced. By relating phenomenology to the descriptions of altered feeling that are found in psychiatry and other contexts, we arrive at the view that all experience incorporates a background feeling of belonging to a world. This background is susceptible to many different kinds of variation, which are gestured at in literature, everyday conversation, psychiatry and elsewhere but have not yet been systematically explored.

Merleau-Ponty, M. (1962) *Phenomenology of Perception.* London: Routledge

Ratcliffe, M. (2008) *Feelings of Being: Phenomenology, psychiatry and the sense of reality.* Oxford: Oxford University Press

Thinking with feeling

Patricia Waugh

T. S. ELIOT PROCLAIMED in *The Use of Poetry and the Use of Criticism* that poetry restores us to the 'deeper unnamed feelings which form the substratum of our being'. This view of poetry is familiar enough, and yet it proposes an entirely different view of knowledge and self-knowledge than what is implicit in the scientific models of understanding which have underpinned the major traditions of Western thought. Here, there is an assumption that to arrive at knowledge of the world and the human self requires the adoption of a transcendent (objective, scientific, rational) 'view from nowhere', a perspective outside of and opposed to the subjective and immanent nature of human

> this is a fascinating time to study consciousness

consciousness. Once mind has been axiomatically detached from body, then affect or emotion, understood as raw bodily experience, or the 'feeling of a feeling', or the colouration of 'mood', are regarded as the major source of human error, deception, unreliability and faulty judgement.

Plato banishes the poets because of their dangerous appeal to the emotions and the body. Stoicism is predominantly preoccupied with rational self-containment as refusal of emotional investment in goods outside of the self. Kantian ethics begins with a suspicion of compassion or sympathy, as feelings arising from a physical body are perceived to be driven by a natural necessity and are therefore inimical to free rational judgement.

Recently, cognitive neuro-science has begun to facilitate a reorientation towards the body which allows for an understanding of the emotions as essential aspects of cognition and of rational judgement, crucial to the processes of consciousness and of understanding what it is to be human.

In English Studies, this 'affective turn' in science is of particular interest because it reorients knowledge towards the kind of understanding which has always been implicit in literary representations and which has also provided the foundation for an appraisal of literary works as important vehicles for ethical understanding and reflection on our processes of judgement. In his seminal work, *The Expression of the Emotions in Humans and Animals* (1872), Charles Darwin first explored the idea that the emotions orient an organism to its environment. Whereas for Plato, only rational knowledge might provide an orientation to the Good, for Darwin, an emotion is a primary judgement on the world which directs our subsequent knowledge of it. Humans are rational beings, but they are also 'dependent rational animals' (in Alastair MacIntyre's phrase) whose flourishing and ethical orientations must evolve out of their particular biological make-up and needs but are mediated and shaped through culture and intersubjective engagement.

Contemporary cognitive neuro-scientists have begun to challenge machinic definitions of consciousness and to argue for a different model of reason. Neuro-scientists such as Antonio Damasio and V. S. Ramachandran have demonstrated ways in which human reason is seriously impaired in brain-damaged patients whose higher cognitive functions are unaffected but who have suffered damage to the emotional centres and the 'limbic' or primitive regions of the brain. Literary theorists, too, are beginning to meditate on the state of 'becoming-animal'. The human being seems caught between the animal and the machine.

Since the Cartesian moment with its emphasis on the disembodied mind, poets and novelists have been seeking ways to represent and explore human consciousness, working with assumptions curiously close to positions now being adopted in contemporary neuro-science. This is a fascinating time to study consciousness, as science is discovering and affirming what poets and novelists have long endeavoured to represent. Many contemporary creative writers, such as Ian McEwan, Kazuo Ishiguro, A. S. Byatt, Tom Stoppard and J. M. Coetzee, have foregrounded these ideas explicitly in recent works. More provocatively perhaps, writers in the late nineteenth and early twentieth centuries were already exploring formal representations of consciousness, sometimes engaging with the ideas of psychologists such as William James, in terms which uncannily anticipate contemporary neuro-scientific and psychological debates.

Damasio, A. (2000) *Descartes' Error: Emotion, reason, and the human brain.* New York: Quill

MacIntyre, A. (2001) *Dependent Rational Animals: Why human beings need the virtues.* New York: Open Court Books

Nussbaum, M. (2001) *Upheavals of Thought: The intelligence of the emotions.* Cambridge: Cambridge University Press

The creativity of scholarship

Penny Wilson

FOR MANY READERS, the address to 'Dulness' put by Alexander Pope into the mouth of the arch-scholar Richard Bentley ('Aristarchus') hits home:

> Like Buoys that never sink into the Flood,
> On Learning's Surface we but lie, and Nod.
> Thine is the genuine Head of many a House,
> And true Divinity without a Nous ...

Indeed, there is a long-standing assumption that 'scholarship' is the opposite of creativity. The very word 'scholar' can conjure up images of people of dry and myopic purpose tracking their way through landscapes of genius. Think of George Eliot's Mr Casaubon, that 'Bat of erudition', of whom Eliot writes: 'With his taper stuck before him he forgot the absence of windows, and in bitter manuscript remarks on other men's notions about the solar deities, he had become indifferent to the sunlight.' But the criticism of Casaubon is the more pointed for coming from a woman who well knew the delights of days and months spent in the minutiae of research. At crucial moments in *Middlemarch*, we are invited to see Casaubon from the viewpoint of the 'intense consciousness within him'; if Eliot is being critical of his misdirected energies, she sees in them traces of a larger vision gone tragically awry. Alexander Pope's variously inventive attacks on scholarship are comparable. Pope devoted ten years to translating and commenting on Homer, and his renunciation of scholarship as pedantry is the more emphatic for his sense that 'the itch of criticism', as he called it in a letter, is part and counterpart of literary creation.

Such contempt for scholarly 'drudgery' has had a major impact on intellectual and cultural history. Huge swathes of human endeavour have been relegated to virtual invisibility on the scale of creativity and 'genius'. Today, the signs of the breaking-down of this ancient opposition, or prejudice, are all around. Scholarship and science are reclaiming their right to the energies of genius, individuality, and transformation. Parameterised computing morphs into performance art presenting the beauty of mathematical braids; glaciologists and biologists of the British Antarctic Survey seek to incorporate and interact with the reactions of painters and writers to the same scenes. What these synergies show is that the gap between rigorous endeavour, scientific practice and individual genius is not as great as once thought. They are all far too interwoven to be separated out into a creativity versus scholarship dualism. The challenge now is to explore the creative forces present in so-called works of learning.

> parameterised
> computing morphs
> into performance art

As inspiration and starting-point one might turn – between Pope and George Eliot – to the suggestive case of William Hazlitt's elegiac celebration of his own father's life among the Biblical commentators. On the one hand we see the study-bound scholar poring with 'lack-lustre' eyes over his dusty and neglected tomes; on the other the 'glimpses' and 'glimmering notions' of camels, palm-trees and the Twelve Tribes which lead in turn to mighty speculations on the age of the world and its predicted end.

Barney, S. A. (ed.) (1991) *Annotation and its Texts.* Oxford: Oxford University Press

Grafton, A. (1990) *Forgers and Critics: Creativity and duplicity in Western scholarship.* Princeton: Princeton University Press

Koestler, A. (1964) *The Act of Creation.* New York: The Macmillan Company

Concrete logic

Boris Wiseman

WHEN JOHN LOCKE ARGUED that one should not think of
snow as *being* white but as *causing* whiteness, in much the same
way that fire causes pain, he raised a fundamental and still open
question about the relationship between the subjective and
objective dimensions of experience. The answer to the question
is proving to be elusive. However, for the social sciences – and
indeed critical theory and aesthetics – the question matters
more than the answer. It brings to light the many thought-
worlds with which human beings have
populated the space between sensible
reality and the perceiving subject, the
environment and the self, snow and the
idea of snow. Said differently, an explora-
tion of *qualia* (subjective sensations) has much to offer to contemporary theory, in particular social theory. The feminist
anthropologist Françoise Héritier has revealed, for example,
that bodily humours – blood, milk, semen, sweat, saliva – are
important sites of inscription of social differences and
hierarchies.

> an exploration of
> *qualia* has much to
> offer social theory

Héritier's ideas in part elaborate a key concept in Lévi-Strauss's
works, that of 'concrete logic', for Lévi-Strauss the mainspring
of cultural creation. Concrete logic emphasises the fact that we
think 'in' and indeed 'with' the sensible world. A good example
is totemic thought. Why does one Amerindian clan adopt the
name Eaglehawk and another the name Crow? One answer is
that the differences between these two species – the Eaglehawk

and the Crow are both carnivores but the former is a predator, the latter a scavenger – may be used to say something about the relationship between the two eponymous clans, namely, that they are at once allies and opponents. Totemism highlights the more fundamental process, at the very source of the institution of a social order, whereby systems of similarities and differences apprehended in nature become the support for thinking the relationship between humans and non-humans (animals are like us, in as much as they are sentient beings, but also different) and, by extension, that between self and human other. Concrete logic relocates elemental thought-processes outside the confines of the mind, and recognises the importance of the dynamic interaction of mind and world for the development of symbolic systems.

What Lévi-Strauss excavates, however, is not *a* logic of the sensible (one needs to get beyond his theory of totemic thought) but, in fact, three distinct logics: a logic of sensible qualities proper, based on such oppositions as raw/cooked, fresh/rotten; a logic of forms, based on such oppositions as empty/full, container/contained, internal/external; and a logic of temporal intervals, based on such oppositions as long/short (= daily/seasonal), cyclical/serial. As the philosopher Claude Imbert observes, Lévi-Strauss offers an alternative 'adherent' logic that underpins and predicates our other ties to the world, one that reunites the qualitative and quantitative at the very root of what makes us human and producers of symbolic systems. As Lévi-Strauss remarks about certain totemic symbols: plants are not only 'good to eat' but 'good to think with'. Beyond the extraction of an immanent logic from the sensorium, Lévi-Strauss's thought points towards a broader programme for sensory studies, one that opens social and aesthetic theory to historical and cross-cultural explorations of the way we constantly reinvent our sensory world.

Imbert, C. (2005) *Maurice Merleau-Ponty*. Paris: Association pour la diffusion de la pensée française

Lévi-Strauss, C. (1966) *The Savage Mind*. London: Weidenfeld and Nicolson

——— (1973) *Introduction to a Science of Mythology*, vol. 2, *From Honey to Ashes*. Translated by John and Doreen Weightman. London: Cape

Back to the Golden Age: engaging with Shari'a

Michael Bohlander

THE ISLAMIC WORLD is changing, slowly but perceptibly. In the next decades it will be vital to understand the dichotomy between the streams of thought underlying the revival of Islamic Shari'a as the central part of many legal systems in the Islamic world, and the struggle of more secular countries such as Turkey to prevent an Islamisation of their legal systems. There is a widespread desire to return to the purity of the roots of Islamic principles in order to be able to give a specific Islamic

> how can one balance divine commands against humanist values?

answer to the manifold issues the modern world faces. This has nothing to do with revisionism. It is about finding one's own identity and casting off clichés ascribed to Islam throughout history.

A non-hysterical response in the West would begin by lawyers entering into a professional dialogue with colleagues in the Muslim world, free from stereotypes and misconceptions, in order to fully understand the complexity of Islamic Law and its tensions with concepts of the Rule of Law as understood in the West, such as freedom of expression and equality of the sexes. These tensions must be solved, yet we cannot solve what we do not understand. Islamic ideas should be properly represented on the international level – after all, we cannot simply blot out over one billion people and the countries they live in when it comes to deciding what the law of the international community should be. Muslims must understand that there are values which the West cannot negotiate. Too often research is hampered either by unwillingness based on prejudice, or by inability based on a lack of professionalism as well as barriers of language and mentality – and that applies to both sides of the dialogue. Much of the non-Muslim research into Islamic law has hitherto been done by non-lawyers, such as political scientists and historians; in the Muslim world there is a predominance of research by Shari'a scholars and a lack of critical or even comparative academic legal studies. The focus has not been on common legal features or differences, but more on policy-oriented angles. Talking about policies is useless if one does not understand the way the system works in reality.

Take a look at Shari'a criminal law, derided and feared by the West for its draconian penalties said to be based on divine revelation. Shari'a presents Western approaches to criminal law with principles that many might consider a violation of the traditional understanding of the Rule of Law. How, for example, can one balance divine commands against humanist values? Classic Shari'a allows for actions to be regarded as offences in judicial cases when they do not meet the criteria for the most serious class based directly in the Qur'an; for Westerners a clear violation of the legality principle. However, in the eyes of Islamic legal scholars, this mechanism of analogy is meant as a safety-valve; it prevents too wide an application of strict penalties. Moderate states such as the United Arab Emirates, who recognise this tension, have chosen a middle path by restricting the use of offences by analogy unless they have been laid down previously by law, thus moving towards a Western understanding of the legality principle. However, Shari'a law, with its flexible approach not bound by too much procedure, can provide lessons to Western systems, for example, in restorative justice, when it allows even homicide offences to be regulated by agreement between the offender and the victim's family, through the use of blood money, or *diyya*; where the offender is unknown, *diyya* can even be provided by the State Treasury. Restorative justice has recently come very much into the focus of sociological and criminological research in the West – why not learn from a very different culture?

An Na'im, A. A. (2008) *Islam and the Secular State: Negotiating the future of Shari'a.* Cambridge, MA: Harvard University Press

Kamali, M. H. (2008) *Shari'ah Law: An introduction.* Oxford: Oneworld Publications

Al-Tahir Ibn Ashur, M. (2006) *Treatise on Maqasid al-Shari'ah.* London and Washington: International Institute of Islamic Thought

The theological ground of secularism

Christopher Insole

GLOBAL EVENTS have pushed the question of the relationship between religion and politics to the fore. On the one hand democracy, capitalism and liberalism are heralded with a 'religious' fervour. On the other hand, adherents to traditional religions increasingly perceive 'secular' liberalism as corrosive and hostile to religious belief and practice. This polarisation has led some commentators to predict an apocalyptic clash of civilisations.

In the face of this, the humanities can provide some calm reflection on the presuppositions of liberal society. Much of the energy so far has been directed towards the 'philosophy' underlying politics. It might now be time for the theologian to challenge the pervasive and self-satisfied assumption that liberalism can, and should, entirely eschew issues of transcendence and truth. The founding thinkers of liberalism – such as Hobbes, Locke, Kant and Burke – gave an account of reality that is ordered to a transcendent reason and will. Furthermore, their concern was to relate their thought to theological concerns, not simply to manage 'religion' as an irrational part of human life.

The panoply of liberal commitments and practices – toleration, individualism, rights, the mixed constitution, the separation of powers, the centrality of law – arise from religion, or more explicitly, from theology. To take just a few examples here: law and rights, and toleration.

Human law mirrors and is answerable to God's law. This is the

nerve of the natural law tradition, at the heart of Catholic theology. Thomas Aquinas discerns a structure of law inscribed into
creation. At the pinnacle is God's eternal law that good should
flourish. When human beings reflect on their own condition it
becomes clear that there are universal forms of flourishing.
Therefore, every human being requires
food, shelter, education and fellowship. In
addition, there are things that are always
harmful: torture, hunger, cruelty and
loneliness. These universal truths com-

> the purpose of human law is to secure the common good

prise natural law. Positive human law is answerable to this
natural law. The purpose of human law is to secure the common
good: a state of tranquillity and justice, where those things that
are universally necessary for human flourishing are preserved.
Our concepts of rights and liberties, for many the foundation
of liberal democracy, emerge out of this tradition of natural law
theology.

Toleration, another shibboleth of liberalism, arose not from
secular indifference to religion, but from a refusal of individuals
and communities to compromise their witness to a transcendent truth, alongside an awareness that our access to this truth
is impeded by sin. Understanding the roots of this helps us to
see that 'tolerance' should not be used now as a disguise for an
aggressive secularism, which mirrors some of the more intoler-
ant features of the very 'fundamentalism' it is attempting to
resist.

Religion is sometimes 'tolerated' in a way that religious people
find intolerable. By understanding the theological roots of liberalism, we find another way of conceiving things: not an
approach that tolerates religion for secular reasons; but, rather,
one that tolerates secularity for religious reasons.

Cuneo, T. (ed.) (2005) *Religion in the Liberal Polity.* Notre Dame, IN: University of Notre Dame Press

Murray, J. C. (2005) *We Hold These Truths to be Self-Evident: Catholic reflections on the American proposition.* Lanham, MD: Rowan and Littlefield Publishers

Rawls, J. (1993) *Political Liberalism.* New York: Columbia University Press

Extreme pornography

Clare McGlynn and Erika Rackley

IT SEEMS THAT WE ARE STARTING to talk about pornography again. The 'porn wars' of the 1980s – the battles between
feminists, liberals and conservatives over the nature, potential
harm and legal regulation of pornography – appeared to dissi-
pate in the 1990s. It was almost as if our perceived ability to *do*
something about pornography faded in the face of its increasing ubiquity. However, the conversation is starting again and
change is afoot in the UK because of new
measures criminalising the possession of   **there has been very**
'extreme' pornography. These measures   **little discussion of**
– greeted with acclaim and derision in   **harm to women**
equal measure – demand engagement
with debates about women, harm, pornography, censorship
and freedom of expression. However, while the latter two concepts have indeed been the focus for debate, there has been
very little discussion of harm, especially harm to women.

Why would this be the case? The current definition of extreme
pornography includes pornographic images of bestiality and
necrophilia, as well as depictions of sexual acts which are life-
threatening or likely to result in serious injury to the anus,
breasts or genitals. This will clearly cover so-called 'snuff' films
and other horrific material, such as sexualised depictions of
women hanging by their necks from meat hooks. What it will
not clearly cover, however, are the easily found, and freely
accessible, images on pornographic rape websites.

Far from being harm*less*, these sites encourage and legitimate gaining sexual arousal from forced sex. Those who view extreme pornography will not necessarily commit sexual offences, but their use, and the very existence, of such material sustains a culture in which rape and sexual violence is normalised.

So, what can be done about this? Legally, we need to carve out a middle way, a feminist way, between the extremes of the anti-censorship liberal position and the moral-conservative concern with the moral decline of society. We need to build on the legacy of the anti-pornography campaigners of the 1980s, of Catharine MacKinnon and Andrea Dworkin (1997), by adapting their thinking and focusing on harm for a new age. We need a liberal feminist argument that would see the harm in pornographic rape websites, but would not seek to subject all pornography to legal regulation.

This argument develops Martha Nussbaum's declaration that much pornography 'directly conflicts with the ideas of equal worth and equal protection that are basic to a liberal social order' (2004: 139). It considers again John Stuart Mill's work in the nineteenth century, particularly his *Subjection of Women*. In this way, we can work towards a legal regime regulating extreme pornography, which takes as its focus harm to women, especially pornographic images of rape.

Dyzenhaus, D. (1992) 'John Stuart Mill and the Harm of Pornography', *Ethics* 102: 534–51

MacKinnon, C. and Dworkin, A. (1997) *In Harm's Way*. Cambridge, MA: Harvard University Press

Nussbaum, M. (2004) *Hiding from Humanity – Disgust, shame and the law*. Princeton: Princeton University Press

Irrationality rules

Daniel Read

THE THEORY OF RATIONAL CHOICE is still at the heart of mainstream economics: people are viewed as omniscient, reflective, and optimising. This view has never been widely held outside of economic theory (and it's doubtful that many economists believe it), but economists have maintained the rationality assumption because of their belief that it was approximately correct, and because there were no satisfactory alternative theories. However, due to the contributions of behavioural economists, and now even neuro-economists, the situation is changing rapidly. These disciplines have introduced new empirical methods into economics and shown how the results can be incorporated into theory.

standard economic theories are not even approximately correct

It is now clear that standard economic theories are not even approximately correct. People are myopic rather than omniscient, impulsive rather than reflective, and work to satisfy minimum standards rather than achieve the best possible ones. Nonetheless, it is possible to accommodate these 'deviations from rationality' within the analytical framework of modern economics.

The new empirical methods have their origins in psychology and, increasingly, neuro-science. Countless experiments have been conducted in which people are placed in real-life situations. These experiments show systematic and consequential irrationalities. One of many illustrations of the influence of behavioural and neuro-economics can be seen in our understanding of how people value future outcomes. This has traditionally been described in terms of reverse compound interest: if something is delayed by one year we devalue it by perhaps 4 per cent, if it is delayed by two years we devalue it by slightly more than 8 per cent, and so on. But people actually put a disproportionately high value on things they can have *right now*, and if they cannot have them now the length of the delay matters relatively little. If something is delayed by a few *minutes* we might devalue it by perhaps 10 per cent, while if it is delayed by two years we devalue it by 12 per cent. We see this in smokers who want to quit but are constantly lighting their 'last' cigarette – future cigarettes matter little, and they promise to avoid them, but the cigarette now is vital. Many behavioural experiments show this, and now neurological studies are beginning to show that the brain reacts differently to immediately available rewards than to delayed ones.

When people are choosing between options and some are immediately available, their amygdala (the part of the brain associated with emotional memory) is much more active than when all of the rewards are delayed. It appears that we treat immediate payoffs as 'primary' rewards and get very excited about them, and that this is hard-wired into the brain and must be accommodated in any theory of human behaviour.

Such compelling evidence has led to revolutionary changes in economic theory, with complicated-looking equations that formerly contained the compound interest assumption now routinely containing *present-biased* preferences. The change looks small, but it has momentous consequences. For example, present-biased preference can explain social problems like obesity, addiction and under-saving. This is only one example, but it does illustrate the goal of behavioural economics and neuro-economics, which is to ground economic thinking in the real world of experience and behaviour.

Cassidy, J. (2006) 'Mind Games', *New Yorker* 18 September 2006

Gilbert, D. (2007) *Stumbling on Happiness*. London: HarperCollins

Read, D. (2007) 'Time and the Marketplace', *Marketing Theory* 7: 59–74

Inflammatory labelling

Alec Ryrie

RECENT RESEARCH on inter-Christian violence in the Reformation age has implications for parallel events in the modern world. This research questions the 'democratic fallacy': the modern assumption that majorities matter. Committed and well-organised minorities can have an impact out of all proportion to their numbers. Even if religious violence is the work of a minority, the quality of dissent matters much more than the quantity. This is doubly so if a 'moderate' majority is disorientated or uncertain. Recent work on the Reformation era underlines that some 'moderation' can be self-defeating. While Protestantism was advancing, leading Catholic clergy from Scotland to Cologne to Hungary attempted to forge compromises with it. Yet this attempt to introduce some Protestant ideas into Catholicism served principally to introduce confusion and to make it extremely difficult to hold the line against further change.

> the purpose of religious violence is often to provoke anger

The language of 'moderation' and 'extremism' was itself dangerous, because committed believers rarely wished to be 'moderate' or lukewarm in their faith. In the sixteenth century, those who advocated moderation were often accused of trying to compromise between good and evil. Labelling religious movements as 'extremist' ironically helped to legitimise them, not least by providing them with the aura of persecution and martyrdom.

While Catholicism was wrestling with self-doubt and compromise, the uncompromising Protestant minority successfully cut short attempts at dialogue through highly visible, strategic and symbolic acts of violence. In France, the Netherlands and Scotland these took the forms of armed public assemblies in defiance of the law, and of the destruction of Catholic church furnishings and images. Importantly, the precise forms of religious violence were governed as much by religious as by pragmatic considerations. The purpose of this violence, even at its bloodiest, was largely demonstrative and theatrical. Its effect was to provoke Catholic counter-attacks, to entrench religious division and to force 'moderates' to choose sides.

Analogies with modern religious conflicts cannot be precise. Yet study of past religious strife raises important questions about how conflict can be managed, and violence deflected, in the modern world. One central lesson is the need to contest the claim of so-called 'extremists' to rigour and purity, which is in part a matter of avoiding terms such as 'extremist' or 'radical'. Violent forms of religion are often better described as 'innovations' or 'distortions', as against 'traditional', 'original', 'authentic' or 'pure' forms of a religious tradition. A deeper problem relates to the role of violence. The purpose of religious violence is often to provoke anger, to forestall compromise and to force potential sympathisers to decide which side they are on. This is powerfully reinforced when those threatening violence are able to portray themselves as persecuted or as martyrs. Dramatic reactions or over-reactions to acts of violence are self-defeating. Nonchalance, weariness, contempt or ridicule, rather than fury, are better able to deflate conflict.

Davies, N. Z. (1975) 'The Rites of Violence' in her *Society and Culture in Early Modern France*. Palo Alto, CA: Stanford University Press

Racaut, L. and Ryrie, A. (eds.) (2005) *Moderate Voices in the European Reformation*. Aldershot: Ashgate

Walsham, A. (2006) *Charitable Hatred: Tolerance and intolerance in England, 1500–1700*. Manchester: Manchester University Press

Terrorism and international law

Eleanor Spaventa

THE TERRORIST ATTACKS perpetrated against the United States first, and Spain and the United Kingdom later, have had a deep impact on our societies from all perspectives: the standing of some of our members from religious or political minorities has been weakened; the increase in security has come at the expense of all members of society; and legal guarantees that were considered common currency in post-war Western democracies are under constant challenge from executive and legislative action. These dynamics can be observed at all levels of governance – national, European and international.

However, there is a dramatic difference between action taken at national level and action taken at supranational level. At national level any counter-terrorism policy forms part of debate in local communities; parliaments and the media, providing at least some democratic mandate in deciding how to counteract the terrorist threat. Matters change when counter-terrorism strategies are adopted by the international community: the United Nations Security Council, say, or the European Union. This situation is particularly problematic when international or European law is used by states to adopt strategies which directly affect individuals, in particular through proscription lists which identify, without judicial assessment, individuals and organisations as being associated with terrorism. In some instances, those affected might even see their assets frozen. Any democratic and judicial

> the increase in security has come at the expense of all

accountability is excluded, as states use international and European law instrumentally to evade the systems of checks and balances that limit their power at home.

Traditional notions of democracy are being challenged by new modes of governance which are far removed from the citizen. Traditional rights discourse is being challenged by the rhetoric of the war on terror. As a counter-response, we need a more binding formulation of the rights of personhood independent of the power of communities of states.

Eechout, P. (2007) 'Community terrorist listings, fundamental rights and UN Security Council resolutions', *European Constitutional Law Review* 3: 183

Nesi, G. (ed.) (2006) *International Co-operation in Counter-Terrorism.* Aldershot: Ashgate

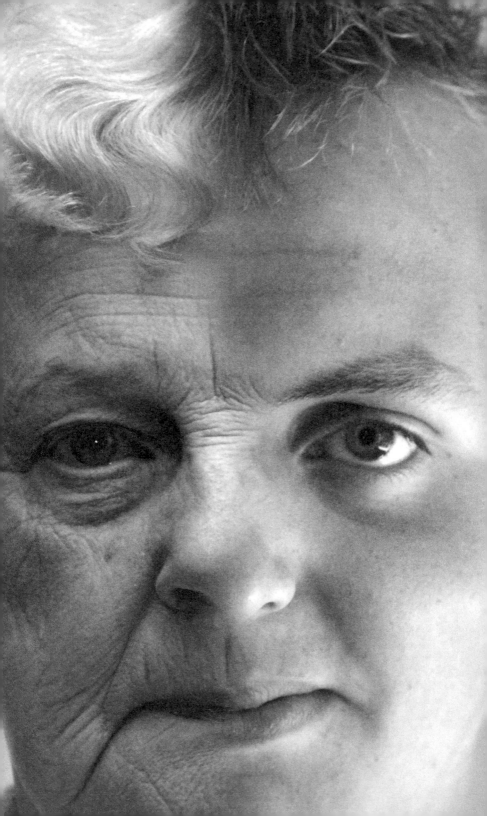

Rule by software

David Budgen

WHEN WE USE our credit cards, make bookings for travel, theatres, concerts, fly on modern aircraft, etc., we are dependent upon the successful working of amazingly complex systems. While new and emerging forms of computing offer ways to cope with the (technical) aspects of complexity, at the same time they can require society to address new issues. Here we examine two examples of such forms and some of the challenges that they present.

Ubiquitous computing is the term used to describe the pervasive use of computers, extending far beyond the current world of the mobile phone, i-Pod and game machines. It encompasses such notions as computers that are controlled by the spoken word, woven into garments, embedded under the skin as implants, and incorporated into yet more of the everyday objects we use.

> we are dependent upon amazingly complex systems

A distinguishing characteristic of such systems is the *autonomous* nature of many of the elements. Each performs its tasks independently, and even more than the Internet, such systems may lack any notion of 'central control'. For such systems, the notion of an overall 'design' is increasingly irrelevant. New elements (and new functionality) can be added at any time – for example, doctors may decide to instruct a wearable garment that is monitoring blood pressure and temperature to begin monitoring a patient's heart-rate as well. However, as so often with 'information systems' in general, the challenges posed by such developments go far beyond the technical. The ability to continuously track the whereabouts of an individual and to monitor intimate details about their physical state raises questions of a more ethical nature. Who should have access to such information and under what conditions? Computer systems whose operation is based upon devolved autonomous 'services' with no sense of any 'central control' will increasingly require society to consider such issues as responsibility, provenance and security as well as how to enforce regulatory constraints.

The computer has also completly changed our attitudes to, and expectations of, the provision of information. Already, the scale of this is progressing beyond the relatively crude access models employed by tools such as Google and similar search engines, which are dependent upon matching of characters within text strings, with no interpretation of their meaning (and hence, for example, no ability to recognise synonyms). Two specific developments are likely to further transform our lives in the 'digital space'. The first is the emergence of the *'semantic web'*, sometimes termed *Web2.0*, intended to provide semantically meaningful access to the Internet and its resources. The second is the ability to *visualise* the information provided and its context (currently apt to be provided in a rather crude form by 'ranked' entries in plain text lists).

Our interest in such information is often described in terms of patterns in some form (I want to find all the books on this topic; the structure of my family tree; how my business may evolve over the next ten years if …). The semantic web will help with posing such questions in a meaningful way – but in exchange our problem of absorbing the information obtained will then be even greater – especially where it relates to abstract, non-physical, forms of knowledge for which we have no shared visual models. Here, we need to draw upon and extend such mechanisms as the ideas about three-dimensional visualisation that are being developed for other purposes. For the present, the dependency upon text acts as a major constraint, and finding better ways of understanding complex patterns of information will enable us to make sensible and convenient use of the rapidly increasing volume and variety of digital information resources.

Berman, F., Fox, G., Hey, A. J. G. and Hey, T. (2003) *Grid Computing: Making the global infrastructure a reality.* New York: John Wiley & Sons

Berners-Lee, T., Hall, W., Hendler, J., Shadbolt, N. and Weitzner, D. J. (2006) 'Creating a Science of the Web', *Science* 313: 769–71

Is the future Asian?

Anoush Ehteshami

WE ARE CURRENTLY WITNESSING the birth of a new epoch, the true twenty-first-century post-Columbian epoch, in which the power wielded by Europe and the United States is coming to an end. The steady shift of influence eastwards suggests progress towards the 'Asianisation' of the international system. Japan's rise in the 1970s and 1980s did not accomplish this for it remained part of a sphere of strategic influence dominated by the United States. Today, China and also India, the drivers of Asianisation, have no such ties to inhibit their global impact. Furthermore, the sheer scale of the changes heralded by the rise of China as a superpower in today's globalised international system is unprecedented.

> the rise of China as a superpower is unprecedented

We are entering what is qualitatively a new age. China has consolidated its position as continental Asia's economic miracle, absorbing large amounts in foreign direct investment and achieving a 10 per cent per year growth rate. By 2000, China's stock of foreign direct investment had stood at $350 billion; its foreign trade at a massive $475 billion, and it had entered the league of the world's top ten exporters. By 2005 the Chinese economy had overtaken those of France and Britain, boasting in the process $1.0 trillion in foreign currency reserves – itself equivalent to the foreign investments of just one tiny West Asian oil exporter, namely Abu Dhabi with 420,000 citizens.

The new powers are creating their own sphere of strategic

influence. Eastern Eurasia is at the centre of a large geo-strategic web. Inter-Asian interaction is fuelling further Asiani-sation, based on energy consumption, Islam as a transnational political force, labour financial movements, and military links; all sustained by the weight of demography (with two-thirds of humanity in situ).

Amineh, M. P. and Houweling, H. (eds.) (2005) *Central Eurasia in Global Politics: Conflict, security and development*. Leiden: Brill

Knutsen, T. L. (1999) *The Rise and Fall of World Orders*. Manchester: Manchester University Press

McDougall, D. (2007) *Asia Pacific in World Politics*. Boulder, CO: Lynne Rienner

Manuscript book, printed book, Facebook

Richard Gameson

DURING THE FOURTH CENTURY AD the scroll (the book of Antiquity) was definitively superseded by the codex – the form of book still current today. In the mid-fifteenth century, Johannes Gutenberg developed printing with movable type, and the hand-operated press remained the basis of publication until mechanisation with steam power in the nineteenth century. From the 1950s other processes that permitted ever more streamlined and economical mass-production superseded movable type itself. More recently, technological advances have revolutionised access to information on an unprecedented scale: electronic publication permits a writer to reach, in principle, an audience of millions with minimal effort and outlay.

At every stage in the long history of the making of books and the transmission of written communication there have been tensions, sometimes explicit, more often implicit, between diffusion, durability, quality and cost. The fourth-century *Codex Sinaiticus* and the copies of Gutenberg's forty-two-line Bible are effectively in as good a condition now as they were the day that they were made. But parchment manuscripts were enormously expensive in terms of raw materials and human labour, while the magnificent forty-two-line Bible was, even in its own day, an extravagant luxury. Conversely, the affordable mass-market paperbacks made in the 1950s are already falling out of their bindings and crumbling to dust.

Gutenberg's invention did not put scribes and illuminators out of business. For a couple of generations, many readers continued to acquire hand-written copies of certain texts for reasons ranging from personal preference through aesthetic attractiveness to convenience. Some of the very finest illuminated manuscripts were in fact made in the later fifteenth and early sixteenth century. Furthermore, early printed books were often decorated by hand, while wood- and metal-cuts offered new opportunities for artists within the printing trade. By contrast, modern progress is not only faster, it is less tolerant of alternatives, and market forces tend to drive older options, whatever their continuing merits, into extinction.

Modern information technology is not outside this paradigm. The longevity of current systems is uncertain: do we really believe that people will be able to consult today's new media 500 years from now, let alone 1,500 – as one can still read Gutenberg's Bible and *Codex Sinaiticus*? Yet the audience for a work stretches through time as well as through space: in the drive to reach as many people as possible *now*, let us not lose sight altogether of future generations. There is also the issue of quality. It is difficult to imagine people a millennium from now marvelling at the best websites of our day in the way that we marvel at masterpieces of medieval calligraphy and illumination such as the *Book of Kells* and the *Lindisfarne Gospels*.

the modern literary letter has already been lost to email

Now this is not a plea and certainly not an argument for turning the clock back: it is simply an invitation to reflect upon the generally overlooked losses that accompany modern communication gains. The Greeks and Romans entrusted their writing to papyrus scrolls whose life expectancy was, they well knew, about 200 years. This is a long time in relation to the life of a human being – and hence wholly acceptable for many purposes – yet it is nothing in terms of the lifetime of humanity (one hopes). Consequently, great civilisations and powers though they were, their literary and documentary remains have largely perished; the main works of Greek and Latin literature that we may read today are, ironically, confined to those texts that happen to have been copied from papyrus scrolls into parchment codices during the Middle Ages.

The modern literary letter, with its vital insights into the life and work – not to mention the handwriting – of our predecessors, has already been all but lost to e-mail. This may be judged a minor sacrifice in relation to the evident gains of cheap, easy and instantaneous global communication. Yet it would be ironic if, in our enthusiasm for diffusing our ideas as widely as possible now, we were to commit overmuch to ultimately transient supports for knowledge, wholly abandoning forms of proven durability; and if consequently our descendants in the fourth millennium should be able to read thoughts, theorems and literary remains extending from the early middle ages up to the early twenty-first century but not from earlier, nor from subsequent periods.

Clanchy, M. T. (1993) *From Memory to Written Record*, 2nd ed. Oxford: Blackwell

Krawietz, P., et al (2000) *Gutenberg, Man of the Millennium: From a secret enterprise to the first media revolution.* City of Mainz

The British NHS: back to the future?

David J. Hunter

THE BRITISH NHS TURNED SIXTY in July 2008. The great survivor is in reasonable shape notwithstanding batterings from continuous reorganisation since the mid-1970s. There is no perfect health system anywhere in the world and the NHS is no exception, although it is acknowledged to be considerably less imperfect than many. In comparative league tables, it is generally seen to perform well and significantly better than the US, which performs poorly and at much higher cost.

The values of collectivism and solidarity that are common to many health systems, especially in Europe, are under threat, challenged by market forces with their focus on competition and choice. The impact and implications of a consumer-led health service are hotly contested. Advocates believe that health services cannot be exempt from more general societal trends in favour of individual choice and responsibility. They also consider that many

> there is no perfect health system anywhere in the world

inequities in health systems are the result of people being unable to exercise choice and subject to a form of professional paternalism. Choice is therefore empowering and good for an individual's self-esteem and confidence.

Opponents of choice and competition believe that health care is unlike other goods and services, especially when it comes to the issue of information asymmetry, and that the need for professionals to make decisions on behalf of sick people remains essential. Furthermore, choice can be stressful and result in ill-health if people believe they may have made the 'wrong' choice or cannot decide in their best interests. Far from choice strengthening social cohesion and risk-pooling, it seems likely to threaten it and widen inequalities.

Perhaps a more useful alternative to consumerism is the notion of co-production. It demands a rebalancing of the relationship between service users and professionals to ensure that it is one of co-equals. As co-producers, users must share more actively both in defining their problems and in devising solutions than they have in the past. With the prevalence of chronic disease, where users are central to its management, a co-production model has appeal and is the basis of successful doctor–patient relationships.

The other major development confronting health systems globally, including the NHS, is the changing nature of disease. Infectious diseases have not disappeared and, in some cases, may be reappearing. But the principal challenges confronting the NHS, and influencing its future cost, are chronic diseases, sometimes called 'diseases of comfort'. With nearly 60 per cent of the UK population predicted to be obese by 2050, resulting in a sevenfold increase in health-care costs, a priority is reshaping the health system to enable it to cope with the health-related consequences of such diseases, notably diabetes and heart disease. Their causes, as distinct from their symptoms, cannot be tackled through the NHS alone. The solutions are complex and cross-cutting and demand strong and sustainable partnerships across different agencies and levels of government. In many ways, the NHS's considerable strength is its principal weakness. Health is equated with tackling ill-health and doing so mainly in hospitals.

But a paradigm shift is under way to transform the NHS from being a sickness service to one centred on health. In his first major speech on the NHS as prime minister, Gordon Brown stressed the importance of prevention, although he seemed to view this largely in terms of either new drug treatments, access to screening and preventive vaccines or providing individuals with more information, advice and education to encourage them to adopt healthier lifestyles. Welcome though the emphasis on prevention is, the desired improvement in the public's health demands a bolder approach on the part of government. All the evidence suggests that a limited approach focused on changing individual lifestyle through education and behavioural change is unlikely to succeed on its own, and will not bring about the desired paradigm shift. Action is needed at multiple levels – individual, local, regional, national and international. The NHS may be a good place to start given its size – employing over one million people – and its position as a major purchaser of goods and services. But government, both local and national, also has a vital stewardship role to perform since there are some actions that only government can take. The success or otherwise of such a multi-faceted approach to the complex matter of improving the public's health will determine the fate of the NHS, even though many of the actions needed to change the projected health profile of the population lie beyond its reach and will require it to work in partnership with others.

Hunter, D. J. (2008) *The Health Debate*. Bristol: Policy Press

Le Grand, J. (2007) *The Other Invisible Hand*. Princeton: Princeton University Press

Nuffield Council of Bioethics (2007) *Public Health: Ethical issues*. London: Nuffield Council on Bioethics

Housing: risky business?

Susan J. Smith

AS THE SHOCK WAVES from a US lending crisis reverberate across the global economy, the phrase 'safe as houses' acquires a somewhat hollow ring. Housing used to be the one area of life that was isolated from the interlocking risks that define the human condition. But it has turned out to be perhaps the most precarious location of all. Ironically, even as governments move to bail out their banks, in the pecking order of risk-management, the security and sustainability of housing – the quantity of home assets, as distinct from the quality of mortgage debt – occupies a rather lowly position.

In the English-speaking countries of the more developed world, and in a growing number of other societies, housing systems revolve around owner occupation. Between two-thirds and three-quarters of the population in the Anglo-American world own or (more usually) are buying their homes. The result is that most people hold the majority of their wealth as property, and personal debts are routinely rolled into mortgages. So much so that home assets are both the centre-piece of households' wealth portfolios, and a financial buffer to lean on, or borrow against, across the life-course.

But any investment and every style of borrowing comes with risks as well as rewards. For housing, credit risks are the most obvious concern: the dangers of mortgage default, eviction or bankruptcy. Equally significant for home occupiers – but less widely aired – are price risks: the possibility that home values may fall, or fail to keep pace with other investments. These credit and investment risks often go together. Those who want to spend from home equity (as people increasingly do) may find that the market is sticky (so that housing wealth can no longer be 'cashed in' by trading down). At the same time, a resurgence of credit rationing may reduce the flexibility mortgagors once had to 'borrow-up' against the value of their homes.

When large institutions are exposed to this kind of risk in relation to any asset or investment other than housing, they manage it with financial instruments known as 'derivatives'. These are contracts whose values derive from the performance of an underlying asset or index, but which can be traded independently. The word 'derivative' is generally associated with the esoteric world of high finance which, thanks to the crisis of 2007, is shrouded in opprobrium. To be sure, the growth of derivatives trading is a major and recent financial event. From a tiny base in the 1980s, the value of outstanding contracts grew to a staggering US$450 trillion by 2007: nearly ten times the world's combined GDP. But it is important to recognise that the *concept* is over a century old, and that contracts exist to cover everything from pork bellies to silver, from bonds to sulphur dioxide emissions. Only housing is an exception (if we exclude the way home purchase routinely operates as a forward market) and this looks set to change. Notwithstanding its link to the 'd'-word, could this shift be used to mitigate the mix of risks that home buyers currently face?

> for the first time, home buyers can 'sell short'

Some housing economists think so. Consider the position. Today, home buyers have just one option. They must buy both a physical property (the home they love; the housing services they use) *and* the investment vehicle attached to it (the ups and downs of price). But financial engineers can now dismantle this package, so that home buyers can enjoy (and pay for) the housing services element of their home, without carrying all the risks (but also by giving up some of the reward) of the investment component. This is because, in the form of futures, options or swaps, housing derivatives effectively separate the investment returns on housing from the ownership and use of property. By gathering up these returns into a price index – a possibility first aired fifteen years ago – individuals and institutions who were previously excluded from, or averse to, holding whole properties can invest incrementally in a 'synthetic' housing market. That is, they can benefit from house price appreciation without owning a single brick, slate or foundation stone. By the same token, those most at risk from declining prices can take steps to mitigate this: for the first time, home buyers can 'sell short'; they can hedge their housing bets. For example, a first-time buyer who has the whole 'housing+investment' package, but who cannot sustain their mortgage repayments could, in theory, sell off some portion of their future investment returns in return for an income or lump sum to pay off their mortgage arrears.

For the most part, ordinary households do not (and should not) dabble directly in derivatives. But as Yale economist Robert Shiller has often argued, there is no reason, in principle, why they should not be protected by these instruments. Housing derivatives could, in theory, be embedded in retail products, or in housing policy initiatives, in ways that benefit the public. Asian financial markets veteran and derivatives banker Ralph Liu, for example, invented the concept of 'economic renting' through SwapRentSM transactions and their embedded mortgage products, with this in mind. Whether derivatives can deliver this 'free lunch', whether they are better than more traditional financial instruments, whether they are put into practice at all, are all open questions.

Nevertheless, people need somewhere to live. The politics of housing across many world regions for as much as a century mean that this 'somewhere' is the market. And, like it or not, ordinary people have often prospered as a result: housing is the most widely spread of all financial assets; it performs well over the medium term; and it is the only substantial resource in most households' wealth portfolio. But housing markets are uniquely eccentric to the risk-management tools used in practically every other area of asset management. It is tempting to see the problem for home buyers today as one of being drawn too far into the workings of financial markets. But there is equally the possibility that they are not adequately protected by the instruments invented to handle investment risks. So it could be argued that, in a financial world riddled with crises and uncertainty, hard-working home buyers will face a uniquely precarious future if governments, policy-makers and the markets they regulate do not work creatively with the concept of housing derivatives.

Case, Karl E., Shiller, R. J. and Weiss, A. N. (1993) 'Index-based futures and options in real estate', *Journal of Portfolio Management* (winter): 83–92

Quigley, J. (2006) 'Real estate portfolio allocation: the European consumers' perspective', *Journal of Housing Economics* 15: 169–88

Shiller, R. (2003) *The New Financial Order. Risk in the twenty-first century*. Princeton: Princeton University Press

Anyone for immortality?

Robert Song

WHY SETTLE for being human when it might be a whole lot more interesting being post-human? Why put up with the random results of human evolutionary development when we could design ourselves so much better? Indeed, if we have the capacity to improve human beings technologically, surely we also have the moral obligation to do so? Novel possibilities for human physical and cognitive enhancement throw up a phalanx of seemingly new questions. And of all the proposed techniques, the most seductive vision is conjured up by life-extension technologies, which offer the prospect of postponing death itself – perhaps even indefinitely. As bioethicist John Harris writes unblushingly, 'The Holy Grail of enhancement is immortality.'

To understand post-humanism properly, we need to be concerned not only with evaluating the intellectual cogency of its ideas, but also to discover what makes such ideas attractive in the first place: intellectual commitments are often intimately linked to deeper, more existential hopes and fears. Posthumanism should be seen as the natural outworking of a nexus of cultural aspirations and philosophical ideas which might be called the 'Baconian project', after the seventeenth-century philosopher of science Francis Bacon. This great movement of thought and practice has been driven by the twin imperatives of eliminating suffering and maximising the realm of human choice, so as to rid human beings of the unwanted burdens of fate. Philosophically this required abandoning the Aristotelian understanding of natural teleology, and developing a new mechanised conception of nature as raw material for human use.

Of course extraordinary benefits have flowed from this project – imagine life before anaesthetics or antibiotics – but it has also left moderns with an indefinable sense of loss. Standard modern bioethics is not well equipped to address or even recognise this ambivalence, not least because its dominant Kantian and utilitarian heritage is itself a product of the seventeenth-century revolution. The pathos of this situation is revealed with unusual clarity in the efforts of the German social theorist Jürgen Habermas to justify the rejection of positive genetic enhancements within a modernist philosophical framework. Lacking a substantial account of nature, he is unable to make the distinction between the natural and the artificial which his fear of eugenics demands. And perhaps sensing his failure, he finds himself turning to theology for a distinction between Creator and creature, which he thinks expresses truths which cannot easily be captured in philosophical terms.

> how can sickness be integrated into a morally valuable life?

Habermas's acknowledgement of the limits of secular philosophy in this context opens up a more general question about what the conditions of thought might be on the other side of secular reason. It also prompts us to recognise that we may need to think very hard about what has been lost as well as what has been gained in the instrumentalisation of nature, including our own bodily nature. This does not imply that it is the job of theology to rescue a naive distinction between the natural and the artificial, the human and the post-human. Rather, one role of theology – and not just of theology – can be to nudge us to ask a different set of questions. What is the difference between moral imagination and narcissistic fantasy? How are we to find meaning and not simply unspeaking darkness in the suffering we will inevitably face? How can sickness be integrated into a morally valuable life that has come to terms with finitude? How are we to care for each other as vulnerable human beings one with another? Our greatest moral task, in other words, is to learn our own humanity. After all, death unforeseen will ever be a threat, even for 'immortal' post-humans.

Habermas, J. (2003) *The Future of Human Nature*, trans. William Rehg, Max Pensky and Hella Beister. Cambridge: Polity Press

Harris, J. (2007) *Enhancing Evolution: The ethical case for making better people*. Princeton: Princeton University Press

McKenny, G. P. (1997) *To Relieve the Human Condition: Bioethics, technology, and the body*. New York: State University of New York Press

Postscript

IDEAS, SCHOLARSHIP and new ways of thinking are at the heart of any great university. Since universities grew from medieval monasteries they have contributed more to our understanding of the universe, society and what it is to be human than any other group of institutions. Universities provide unique environments for new ideas to germinate; for unpopular ideas to thrive; and for creativity to be nurtured. Universities disseminate new ideas through educating the young and sending them into the world as better people. Who can contemplate how much poorer today's world would be without the ideas in science, social science and the humanities which have emerged from the world's universities?

The very ethos of what defines a university is currently a matter of debate. It is critical that scholarship, education, and thinking about better ways of living and doing things are all central to what a university should be. We should not confuse 'teaching' – repackaging and dissemination of existing ideas – with education and scholarship, which generate new ideas and open the minds of leaders of the future. It is no accident that one of the first targets of any extremist regime is the university. The ideas it generates are central to the future of our civilisation and society.

Durham has been a leading place of scholarship for a millennium. Durham Cathedral is the burial place of the Venerable Bede, the greatest European scholar of the seventh to eighth century. The religious, scholarly community in Durham in the thirteenth century founded Balliol, University and Trinity

Colleges in Oxford and, in Durham itself, evolved into England's third university.

If you have read to this point, you will, no doubt, have dipped into the real content of this book. Researchers from across the disciplinary base at Durham University have tried to provide a snapshot of what universities are about and for – and where the world may be heading. I hope it has enriched your thinking, stimulated an appreciation of what universities should be about, and helped to show how ideas can change thinking about the world.

Professor Christopher Higgins

About the contributors

Ash Amin

Ash Amin is Professor of Geography and Executive Director of the Institute of Advanced Study at Durham University. He is a Fellow of the British Academy. He writes on topics at the intersection of society and space relating to local futures in a global economy, the geography of the knowledge economy, the challenges of multiculturalism, and politics in a post-territorial age. His most recent books include *Cities: Reimagining the Urban* (with Nigel Thrift, Polity Press, 2002), *Architectures of Knowledge* (with Patrick Cohendet, Oxford University Press, 2004), *Community, Economic Creativity and Organisation* (edited with Joanne Roberts, Oxford University Press, 2008) and *The Social Economy* (edited, Zed Press, London, forthcoming). ash.amin@durham.ac.uk

Colin Bain

Professor Colin Bain is Director of Research in Chemistry at Durham University and a director of the Institute of Advanced Study. His research interests lie in surface chemistry and optical physics. (see www.colinbain.net) c.d.bain@durham.ac.uk

Mike Bentley

Dr Mike Bentley is a glacial geologist working as a reader in the Department of Geography at Durham University. He carries out research on past changes in the West Antarctic Ice Sheet. He has spent eight summer seasons in the Antarctic, working closely with the British Antarctic Survey. Recent research projects include a study of an Antarctic ice shelf, using sediments deposited at the edge of the ice shelf to determine its history for the last 10,000 years; and ongoing projects to find out how several sectors of the West Antarctic Ice Sheet have thinned since the end of the last ice age. He was recently awarded the W. S. Bruce Medal for his contribution to polar research. m.j.bentley@durham.ac.uk

Tim Blackman

Tim Blackman is Professor of Sociology and Social Policy at Durham University and Director of the University's Wolfson Research Institute. His current research is concerned with how to tackle complex social policy issues, especially health inequalities, and he works as a government adviser on local health improvement strategies. He is an academician of the Academy of Social Sciences, board director of a social housing company and governor of a local hospital. tim.blackman@durham.ac.uk

Michael Bohlander

Before joining Durham University as a professor in 2004, Michael Bohlander was a member of the German judiciary since 1991. From 1999 until 2001 he served as a senior legal officer at the Yugoslavia War Crimes Tribunal. He has trained judges and prosecutors from Egypt, Palestine, Afghanistan, Kuwait and Iraq, including those of the Iraqi High Tribunal that tried Saddam Hussein. His research focuses mainly on comparative and international criminal law, with a recent emphasis on Islamic criminal justice. He has written six and edited two books and has over a hundred articles, comments and book reviews to his name. His work has been cited by the highest German courts. michael.bohlander@durham.ac.uk

John Bolton

John Bolton has been a pure mathematician at Durham since 1970, and he first met Professor Willmore when he taught a course on calculus which John took as an undergraduate student in Liverpool in 1964. He has studied problems concerning the mathematics of soap-film surfaces. john.bolton@durham.ac.uk

Donna-Marie Brown

Donna-Marie Brown is a lecturer in Geography at Dundee University. Located broadly within the spheres of social, cultural and political geography and urban studies, her research focuses on four interrelated themes: identity, space and politics; theorising the everyday city; urban policy; and qualitative research design and methods. d.m.y.brown@dundee.ac.uk

David Budgen

David Budgen is Professor of Software Engineering at Durham University. Major research interests include software design and empirical software engineering and he is currently leading a project that is seeking to adapt evidence-based practices for software engineering. david.budgen@durham.ac.uk

Kenneth Calman

Kenneth Calman is Chancellor at the University of Glasgow and prior to that was Vice-Chancellor at the University of Durham. His career has been predominantly in medicine, and especially in the field of cancer. He was Chief Medical Officer in Scotland and then in England. He is currently a trustee of the British Library, President of the Institute of Medical Ethics and Chairman of the National Cancer Research Institute.

David Campbell

David Campbell is Professor of Cultural and Political Geography at Durham University, where he serves as an associate director of the Durham Centre for Advanced Photography Studies and Academic Director of the International Boundaries Research Unit. In 2005 he gave the Sem Presser Lecture ('Has "Concerned Photography" a Future?') at the World Press Photo Awards in Amsterdam. David is one of the curators/editors of the 'Imaging Famine' project and is working on a new book which explores the visual economy of geopolitics through the photographic depiction of Sudan in the post-Second World War period. david.campbell@durham.ac.uk

John Chapman

Dr John Chapman is Reader in Archaeology at Durham University, with special interests in Balkan and European prehistory. His studies of material culture focus on the interaction between people, places and objects, more specifically in the use of deliberately broken fragments 'after the break'. j.c.chapman@dur.ac.uk

David E. Cooper

David E. Cooper was Professor of Philosophy at Durham University from 1986 to 2008. He has been a visiting professor at universities in several countries, including the USA, Canada and Sri Lanka. His many books include *World Philosophies* (Blackwell, 1996), *The Measure of Things* (Oxford University Press, 2002) and *A Philosophy of Gardens* (Oxford University Press, 2006). He is currently engaged in Durham University's Projects Sri Lanka and Thailand, and is writing a book on Buddhism and beauty. d.e.cooper@durham.ac.uk

Sarah Curtis

Sarah Curtis, Professor of Health and Risk at Durham University, is an internationally renowned specialist in the geography of health, focusing on the geographical dimensions of inequalities of health and health care. Her scholarship elucidates how, and why, varying geographical settings relate to human health inequalities. Much of her research has relevance for public policy and involves work with a range of agencies concerned with public health and health care. s.e.curtis@durham.ac.uk

Jon Davidson

Jon Davidson is Professor of Earth Sciences at Durham University. He was a professor at UCLA for twelve years previously, winning the Wager Medal of IAVCEI in 1998. His research has focused on a wide range of earth science topics, from understanding how volcanoes work to the origin of the continental crust. j.p.davidson@durham.ac.uk

Douglas Davies

Douglas Davies – anthropologist and theologian – is Professor in the Study of Religion at Durham University. He recently published *The Theology of Death* (Continuum, 2008), edited *The Encyclopedia of Cremation* (Ashgate, 2005), and wrote *Death, Ritual and Belief* (Continuum, 2002), and *A Brief History of Death* (Blackwell, 2004). The last two works are translated in Italian, and in Japanese and Greek, respectively. Other books cover Mormonism and Anglicanism. He is a Doctor of Letters of Oxford University and an Honorary Doctor of Theology from Uppsala in Sweden. douglas.davies@durham.ac.uk

Shari Daya

Shari Daya was until September 2008 a research associate in Geography at Durham University. She is now Lecturer in Human Geography at the University of Cape Town. Since completing her PhD in 2006 she has explored the politics of modernity through a range of research projects. Recent publications include 'Embodying modernity: reading narratives of Indian women's sexual autonomy and violation' (*Gender, Place and Culture,* forthcoming), 'Transgressive bodies: textual constructions of the new Indian woman' (*Bound and Unbound: Interdisciplinary approaches to genders and sexualities,* eds. Davy et al., 2008) and a special issue of *Narrative Inquiry* entitled 'Power and Narrative' (co-edited with Lisa Lau). shari.daya@uct.ac.za

Anoush Ehteshami

Anoush Ehteshami is Professor of International Relations and Head of the School of Government and International Affairs at Durham University. He has also been a fellow of the World

Economic Forum. He was Vice-President of the British Society for Middle Eastern Studies (BRISMES) 2000–3. a.ehteshami@durham.ac.uk

Aidan Feeney

Aidan Feeney is a senior lecturer in the Department of Psychology and is interested in how we think. He has published papers on how children and adults make generalisations, on the relationship between thinking and emotion, and on how our beliefs affect how we test hypotheses. aidan.feeney@durham.ac.uk

Charles Fernyhough

Charles Fernyhough is a developmental psychologist with a particular interest in Vygotsky's theory of the relation between language and thought. In recent years he has been exploring its implications for psychosis and other forms of psychopathology. His book *The Baby in the Mirror: A child's world from birth to three* is published by Granta (2008). c.p.fernyhough@durham.ac.uk

John Findlay

John Findlay is a professor at the University of Durham (Emeritus from his retirement in 2007) and Director of the Durham Research Centre for Vision and Visual Cognition. He is a fellow of the British Psychological Society. His research has contributed to an understanding of how oculomotor processes (eye movements) are integrally involved in active vision. His academic career has been based in Durham, with research fellowships at Paris, Toronto, Munich, Bristol and Auckland. j.m.findlay@durham.ac.uk

Carlos Frenk

Carlos Frenk is the Ogden Professor of Fundamental Physics and Director of the Institute for Computational Cosmology at Durham University. He is one of the originators of the 'cold dark matter' theory for the formation of galaxies and other cosmic structures. He and his research group carry out large cosmological simulations of the universe using the 'Cosmology Machine' at Durham, one of the largest supercomputers in the UK. He has written over 200 scientific papers in refereed journals and has edited two books. He is one of the top ten most cited authors in the world in the scientific literature on Space Sciences and Astronomy. He was elected a Fellow of the Royal Society in 2004 and has played an active role in the dissemination of astronomy and cosmology through the media. He has given several public lectures and, in addition to many radio and newspaper interviews, has appeared on numerous TV programmes.

Richard Gameson

Richard Gameson is Professor of the History of the Book at Durham University. He has published some seventy studies of medieval manuscripts, book collections and cultural history. His most recent books are *Treasures of Durham University Library* (Durham University, 2007) and *The Earliest Books of Canterbury Cathedral* (The British Library Publishing Division, 2008). richard.gameson@durham.ac.uk

Giles Gasper

Giles Gasper is a lecturer in Medieval History in the Department of History at Durham University. The focus of his academic work is the eleventh to thirteenth centuries, with particular interests in the development and evolution of medieval theology, and especially the life, work and legacy of Anselm of Canterbury. The reception of the Fathers, including the Greek Fathers, in high medieval intellectual culture is a second major interest, and a third is the reception of and attitude towards medieval thought in the modern churches. g.e.m.gasper@durham.ac.uk

Nigel Glover

Nigel Glover is Professor of Physics and is the Director of the Institute for Particle Physics Phenomenology at Durham University. He is an expert in the physics of high energy colliders and has published more than a hundred papers in refereed scientific journals. e.w.n.glover@durham.ac.uk

Michael Goldstein

Professor Michael Goldstein (Department of Mathematical Sciences) is a statistician working in the general area of Bayesian statistics. In particular, he has developed a generalised version of this approach, termed Bayes linear statistics, appropriate to the treatment of problems which are much too complex for full uncertainty specification. He has applied this approach extensively in the general area of computer models for large-scale physical systems. michael.goldstein@durham.ac.uk

Stephen Graham

Stephen Graham is Professor of Human Geography at Durham University. He has a background in geography, urban planning and the sociology of technology. His research addresses the links between cities, mobility, infrastructure, technology, surveillance and political violence. His latest book, *Cities Under Siege: The New Military Urbanism*, will be published by Verso in summer 2009. s.d.n.graham@durham.ac.uk

Carol Harrison

Carol Harrison is a reader in Theology at Durham University. Her publications include three books on Augustine: *Beauty and Revelation in the Thought of Saint Augustine* (Clarendon Press, 1992); *Augustine in Context: Christian Truth and Fractured Humanity* (Oxford University Press, 2000) and *Rethinking Augustine's Early Theology: an argument for continuity* (Oxford University Press, 2006). She is editor of the Routledge *Early Church Fathers* series and is currently serving as President of the International Association of Patristic Studies. carol.harrison@durham.ac.uk

Christopher Higgins

Chris Higgins is Vice-Chancellor and Warden of Durham University, the university from which he graduated. Before taking up this post in 2007 he had a distinguished career as a biomedical scientist at the University of California at Berkeley, Dundee University, Oxford University and Imperial College London. He has published over 200 original research articles in areas of cell and molecular biology and microbiology, and received national and international awards for his work on ABC transporters, drug resistance of cancers and cystic fibrosis, including the Fleming medal, CIBA medal and a Howard Hughes International Scholarship. He served as scientific adviser to the House of Lords select committee on stem cells, is a member of the Human Genetics Commission and chairs the government's Spongiform Encephalopathy Advisory Committee (SEAC).

Wolfram Hinzen

Wolfram Hinzen is Professor of Philosophy at Durham University. He specialises in questions of human evolution and the structure of language. His books include *Mind Design and Minimal Syntax* (Oxford University Press, 2006) and *An Essay on Names and Truth* (Oxford University Press, 2007). wolfram.hinzen@durham.ac.uk

Ray Hudson

Ray Hudson is Professor of Geography and Pro-Vice-Chancellor at Durham University. His research centres on the political economy of spatial development and on the materiality of the economy. He holds the degrees of BA, PhD and DSc from Bristol University and an honorary DSc from Roskilde University. A Fellow of the Academy of Social Sciences, the British Academy and Academia Europaea, he was awarded the Victoria Medal by the Royal Geographical Society in recognition of his research. Recent publications include *Producing Places* (Guilford Press, 2001) and *Economic Geographies* (Sage, 2005). ray.hudson@durham.ac.uk

Ifan Hughes

Ifan Hughes is a senior lecturer in Physics at Durham University. His research interests include quantum physics with cold atoms and molecules and nonlinear spectroscopy. He is a member of the Institute of Physics and of the American Physical Society. i.g.hughes@durham.ac.uk

David Hunter

David Hunter is Professor of Health Policy and Management in the School of Medicine and Health at Durham University. He is a fellow of the Wolfson Research Institute. His research interests lie in public health and health inequalities. He is an honorary member of the Faculty of Public Health and a Fellow of the Royal College of Physicians (Edinburgh). He is Chair of the UK Public Health Association. d.j.hunter@durham.ac.uk

Chris J. Hutchison

Chris Hutchison holds a chair in Cell Biology at Durham University. His research interests span the structure and function of the cell nucleus and how adult stem cells influence organismal ageing. He has won a number of awards for his research, including an MRC senior fellowship award (1989), a Wellcome Trust Research Leave Fellowship (1994) and a Raine Foundation Distinguished Professor Award (2003).

Christopher Insole

Christopher Insole is a lecturer in Theology and Ethics at Durham University. His previous publications include *The Politics of Human Frailty: A theological defence of political liberalism* (University of Notre Dame Press, 2005), and *The Realist Hope: A critique of anti-realist approaches in contemporary philosophical theology* (Ashgate, 2006). He is currently writing *Kant and the Divine Mind: A study in theology, cognition and ethics* (forthcoming). christopher.insole@durham.ac.uk

Robert Layton

Robert Layton is Professor of Anthropology at Durham University. He is the author of a number of books and articles covering topics as diverse as: social evolution and social change, especially the place of hunting and gathering and peasant farming in human evolution; art and cognition; indigenous rights; warfare, conflict and civil society. r.h.layton@durham.ac.uk

Keith Lindsey

Keith Lindsey is Director of Research and Professor of Plant Molecular Biology at Durham University's School of Biological and Biomedical Sciences. His research interests are in understanding molecular mechanisms of plant development. He has published over a hundred peer-reviewed research papers and review articles, four patents, has authored one book and edited three in the area of plant science (one with seven supplements) and is a Fellow of the Institute of Biology. He is a member of the UK Government Advisory Committee on Releases to the Environment (ACRE) and, until recently, the Multinational *Arabidopsis* Steering Committee and the BBSRC Steering Committee for *Arabidopsis* Functional Genomics (GARNet). keith.lindsey@durham.ac.uk

Reuben Loffman

Reuben Loffman is a postgraduate student at Keele University who is currently preparing a doctoral thesis concerned with historicising violence in the Democratic Republic of the Congo (DRC). He took his first degree at Lancaster University and subsequently did two MAs, at the London School of Oriental and African Studies (SOAS) and Durham University respectively. r.loffman@ihum.keele.ac.uk

Jane Macnaughton

Jane Macnaughton is a GP (now working mainly in gynaecology) and medical educator who is the Director of Durham University's Centre for Arts and Humanities in Health and Medicine (CAHHM). She was founding secretary of the UK Association for Medical Humanities and joint editor of the journal *Medical Humanities*. She is Honorary Senior Lecturer at the University of Sydney's Centre for Values and Ethics in Medicine and has published in the fields of literature and medicine, health-care environments and medical education. jane.macnaughton@durham.ac.uk

Clare McGlynn

Clare McGlynn is Professor of Law at Durham University and an expert in feminist legal studies. Her books include *Families and the European Union: Law, politics and pluralism* (Cambridge University Press, 2006) and *The Woman Lawyer: Making the difference* (Oxford University Press, 1988). Her current work focuses on crime, gender and law, particularly the regulation of extreme pornography and rape law. clare.mcglynn@durham.ac.uk

Michael O'Neill

Michael O'Neill is Professor of English and a director of the Institute of Advanced Study at Durham University. He has published books, chapters and articles on many aspects of Romantic literature, and on an array of Victorian, twentieth- and twenty-first-century poets. Recent books include *The All-Sustaining Air: Romantic legacies and renewals in British, American, and Irish poetry since 1900* (Oxford University Press, 2007), a co-edited annotated anthology, *Romantic Poetry* (Blackwell, 2007), a co-authored exhibition catalogue, *Dante Rediscovered*

(Wordsworth Trust, 2007) and a collection of poems, *Wheel* (Arc, 2008). m.s.o'neill@durham.ac.uk

David Over

David Over is a professor in the Department of Psychology at Durham University. Trained as a philosophical logician, David has collaborated with psychologists for many years. He is interested in the relationship between decision-making and reasoning and has published many papers on how people think about conditionals. david.over@durham.ac.uk

Max Paddison

Max Paddison is Professor of Music Aesthetics at Durham University. He has published widely on the philosophy and sociology of nineteenth- and twentieth-century music, the avant-garde and rock music, and is author of *Adorno's Aesthetics of Music* (Cambridge University Press, 1993; reprinted 1997), and *Adorno, Modernism and Mass Culture* (Kahn & Averill, 1996; rev. ed. 2004). He is joint editor (with Irène Deliège) of the book *Contemporary Music: Theoretical and philosophical perspectives* (Ashgate, 2008). m.h.paddison@durham.ac.uk

Joe Painter

Joe Painter is Professor of Geography and Director of the Centre for the Study of Cities and Regions at Durham University. His research interests include: urban and regional politics and governance; the changing nature of the state, citizenship and democracy; and theories of space, place and territory. He is the co-author of *Practising Human Geography* (Sage, 2004) and of *Political Geography: An introduction to space and power* (Sage, 2009). j.m.painter@durham.ac.uk

David Parker

David Parker is Professor of Chemistry at Durham University. He has received many prizes, including the Corday-Morgan Medal and Prize in 1989, the ICI Prize in Organic Chemistry in 1991, the RSC Interdisciplinary Award in 1996, the inaugural IBC Award for Supramolecular Science and Technology in 2000, the first RSC award for Supramolecular Chemistry in 2002, and a Tilden lectureship and Silver Medal in 2003. In 2002 he was elected a Fellow of the Royal Society. david.parker@durham.ac.uk

Graham Philip

Graham Philip is Professor of Archaeology at Durham University. He researches the later prehistory and Bronze Ages of the east Mediterranean basin. He has particular interests in landscape studies, material culture and the organisation of small-scale complex societies. He currently directs a joint British-Syrian landscape project in the Orontes Valley region of western Syria, and is editor of the journal *Levant*. graham.philip@durham.ac.uk

Roy Quinlan

Roy Quinlan was appointed as Professor of Biomedical Sciences at Durham University in 2001. He is a cell biologist researching those minute (10nm – or a millionth of a centimetre) filaments that determine the shape and function of individual cells and how they are integrated into tissues such as the eye lens. He is Deputy Director of the Biophysical Sciences Institute, which was formed in 2007. r.a.quinlan@durham.ac.uk

Erika Rackley

Erika Rackley is a lecturer in the Law School at Durham University. Her research interests lie primarily in the role of the imagination in shaping and informing understandings of law, justice and adjudication, with a strong emphasis on feminist/gender perspectives. She is co-convenor, with Clare McGlynn, of the research group 'Gender & Law at Durham' (GLAD). erika.rackley@durham.ac.uk

Matthew Ratcliffe

Matthew Ratcliffe is a reader in Philosophy at Durham University. Most of his recent work addresses issues in phenomenology, philosophy of psychology and philosophy of psychiatry. He is author of *Rethinking Commonsense Psychology: A critique of folk psychology, theory of mind and simulation* (Palgrave, 2007) and *Feelings of Being: Phenomenology, psychiatry and the sense of reality* (Oxford University Press, 2008). m.j.ratcliffe@durham. ac.uk

Daniel Read

Daniel Read is Professor of Behavioural Economics at Durham University Business School. He has studied variety-seeking (how consumers choose to diversify consumption), intertemporal choice (how people trade off current and future consumption), and decision-making under risk. He has written many papers on theoretical issues in decision-making. Current work includes a formal model of intertemporal choice, and a study of the causes of and solutions to cost overruns in major projects. daniel.read2@durham.ac.uk

Stephen Regan

Stephen Regan is Professor of English at Durham University, where he is also Director of the Basil Bunting Centre for Modern Poetry. His publications include *Irish Writing: An anthology of Irish writing 1789–1939* (Oxford University Press, 2004) and *Irelands of the Mind: Memory and identity in modern Irish culture* (Cambridge Scholars Press, 2008). stephen.regan@durham.ac.uk

Richard Reid

Dr Richard Reid was Lecturer in African and Imperial History at Durham University from 2002 until 2007. He is presently Lecturer in the History of Africa at the School of Oriental and African Studies, University of London. He is the author of *Political Power in Pre-Colonial Buganda* (James Currey, 2002), *War in Pre-Colonial Eastern Africa* (Ohio University Press, 2007), and *A History of Modern Africa: 1800 to the present* (Blackwell, 2008). He has also written numerous articles on various aspects of violence and militarism in northeast Africa, with particular reference to Ethiopia and Eritrea. He continues to work on the origins and nature of warfare in African history. rr15@soas.ac.uk

Jonathan Rigg

Jonathan Rigg is Professor of Geography at Durham University, specialising in agrarian change and the development process in the Asian region. His fieldwork has largely been in mainland Southeast Asia, particularly Thailand, Laos and Vietnam. Jonathan is interested in revealing how 'ordinary' people respond and adapt to the opportunities and challenges created by rapid economic and social change. His most recent books have been *An Everyday Geography of the Global South* (Routledge, 2007), *Living with Transition in Laos* (Routledge-Curzon, 2005), and *Southeast Asia: the human landscape of modernisation and development* (Routledge, 2003). j.d.rigg@durham.ac.uk

Charlotte Roberts

Charlotte Roberts is Professor of Archaeology at Durham University. She researches the history of disease in archaeological human remains. Please see her web page for full details of her research interests, publications and current research projects. http://www.dur.ac.uk/archaeology/staff/?id=163

Christopher Rowe

Christopher Rowe is Professor of Greek and was until recently Head of the Department of Classics and Ancient History in Durham University, having previously been H. O. Wills Professor of Greek at the University of Bristol. His publications have been mainly on Plato (including commentaries on five dialogues) and Aristotle (including a new translation of the *Nicomachean Ethics*). He is a former president of the International Plato Society and of the Hellenic Society, and is a Fellow both of the Society of Antiquaries and of the Higher Education Academy. c.j.rowe@durham.ac.uk

Alec Ryrie

Alec Ryrie is a reader in Church History in the Department of Theology and Religion at Durham University. He works on the history of the Reformation in the British Isles, with a particular interest in the development of Protestantism in England and

Scotland. His books include *The Gospel and Henry VIII* (Cambridge University Press, 2003), *The Origins of the Scottish Reformation* (Manchester University Press, 2006) and *The Sorcerer's Tale: Faith and fraud in Tudor England* (Oxford University Press, 2008). alec.ryrie@durham.ac.uk

Chris Scarre

Chris Scarre is Professor of Archaeology at Durham University where his primary research interests lie in the early farming communities and megalithic monuments of Atlantic Europe. He has directed field projects in France, Portugal and (most recently) the Channel Islands, and is editor of a leading textbook of world prehistory, *The Human Past* (Thames & Hudson, 2005). chris.scarre@durham.ac.uk

Ray Sharples

Ray Sharples FRAS is Professor of Physics and the Director of the Centre for Advanced Instrumentation at Durham University. He has been a practising observational cosmologist for nearly thirty years. His research into distant galaxies requires measurements of extremely faint sources which can only be made at observing sites with the very darkest skies on Earth. r.m.sharples@durham.ac.uk

Susan J. Smith

Susan J. Smith is Professor of Geography and a director of the Institute of Advanced Study at Durham University. She is a Fellow of the British Academy, a Fellow of the Royal Society of Edinburgh and a member of the Academy of Social Sciences. Her research on the integration of housing, mortgage and financial markets is funded by the UK's Economic and Social Research Council, as part of its Professorial Fellowship Scheme (RES-051-27-0126). Drawing on qualitative methods alongside more conventional quantitative tools, this work documents the changing character of the housing economy: the ups and downs of price; the janus-face of mortgage debt; and the challenge of mitigating housing risk. susanj.smith@durham.ac.uk

Robert Song

Robert Song is a senior lecturer in Christian Ethics in the Department of Theology and Religion at Durham University. He has published widely in theological ethics, including *Christianity and Liberal Society* (Clarendon Press, 1997) and *Human Genetics: Fabricating the Future* (Darton, Longman and Todd, 2002). He has interests in social and political theology, bioethics and medical ethics, and is currently working on a book on the theological foundations of bioethics. robert.song@durham.ac.uk

Eleanor Spaventa

Eleanor Spaventa is a reader in Law at Durham University and Director of the Durham European Law Institute. Her research interests lie in European law and in particular in the fields of European constitutional law, free movement, fundamental rights and cooperation in criminal matters in the EU. She has published extensively in these areas. She is the author of *Free Movement of Persons in the EU – Barriers to movement in their constitutional context* (Kluwer Law International, 2007); the co-author of Wyatt and Dashwood's *European Union Law* (Sweet and Maxwell, 2006), and the co-editor of *Social Welfare and EU Law* (Hart, 2005). She is a recognised expert in European law and has been invited by the House of Lords Constitutional

241

Committee to submit evidence on the new Treaty of Lisbon.
eleanor.spaventa@durham.ac.uk

Paul Stephenson

Paul Stephenson is a reader in Medieval History and was formerly Rowe Professor of Byzantine History at the University of
Wisconsin. He is author of *Byzantium's Balkan Frontier* (Cambridge University Press, 2000), *The Legend of Basil the Bulgar-
slayer* (Cambridge University Press, 2003) and two works
forthcoming in 2009: *The Byzantine World,* and *Constantine.*

James Stirling

James Stirling CBE FRS is the Jacksonian Professor of Natural
Philosophy in the Cavendish Laboratory at Cambridge University. His research area is theoretical particle physics. He has
published more than 300 research papers, including some of
the most frequently cited papers in the physical sciences. His
particular research interest is particle physics phenomenology
– the interface between theory and experiment – and he works
closely with experimentalists at research laboratories in Europe
and the United States. In recognition of his contribution to
particle physics research he was elected to the Fellowship of the
Royal Society in May 1999. He was a director of the Institute
of Advanced Study and Pro Vice-Chancellor for Research at
Durham until late 2008.

Jamie Tehrani

Jamie Tehrani is an RCUK-sponsored research fellow at the
Department of Anthropology at Durham University. His work
focuses on how the processes by which people acquire, modify

and pass on their knowledge and skills produce the kinds of cultural patterns that are documented in the archaeological and ethnographic records. jamie.tehrani@durham.ac.uk

Maurice Tucker

Maurice Tucker is Professor of Geological Sciences and Master of University College at Durham University, following appointments at the Universities of Newcastle, Berkeley, Cardiff and Sierra Leone. He was President of the International Association of Sedimentologists (1998–2002), and of the European Union of Geosciences. He is a fellow of the Academy of Arts and Science of Croatia, and has received medals from the Geological Societies of London and Belgium. He has published over a hundred papers on limestones and written three standard textbooks on sedimentary rocks. m.e.tucker@durham.ac.uk

Patricia Waugh

Patricia Waugh is Professor of English at Durham University. She has written extensively on modern literature, aesthetics, literary theory and modernism and post-modernism. Her most recent publications include, as editor, *Literary Theory and Criticism: an Oxford guide* (Oxford University Press, 2006). She is currently completing a monograph, *The Blackwell History of the British and Irish Novel 1945–present*, and is also working on a monograph, *Literature, Science and the Good Society*, on the two cultures debate (to be completed in 2009), examining engagements between literary and scientific cultures from the late nineteenth century to the present. p.n.waugh@durham.ac.uk

Tony Wilkinson

Tony James Wilkinson is Professor of Archaeology at Durham University. He is a Fellow of the British Academy. His research interests include: the archaeology of the Middle East landscape; long-term trends in settlement and population; geoarchaeology, and human impacts on the environment. His book *Archaeological Landscapes of the Near East* (University of Arizona Press, 2003) was awarded the Society for American Archaeology Book Award (2004) and the James R. Wiseman Book Award of the Archaeological Institute of America (2005). t.j.wilkinson@durham.ac.uk

Penny Wilson

Penny Wilson is Principal of Ustinov College, Durham's postgraduate college. She is also a reader in English, and an Emeritus Fellow of New Hall, Cambridge. She has published widely on eighteenth-century literature and on the reception of the Classics, and is currently working on a book on commentary. p.b.wilson@durham.ac.uk

Boris Wiseman

Boris Wiseman is a senior lecturer in the School of Modern Languages and Cultures and was an inaugural Fellow of the Institute of Advanced Study at Durham University. His research is concerned with various forms of interdisciplinary connections, in particular that between anthropology and aesthetics. He is the author of *Lévi-Strauss, Anthropology and Aesthetics* (Cambridge University Press, 2007) and the editor of *The Cambridge Companion to Lévi-Strauss* (Cambridge University Press, 2009). He is part of the International Rhetoric Culture project, in the context of which he is co-editing a volume on chiasmus and culture. His current research is concerned with the place of qualia, and more generally the senses, in contemporary social and aesthetic theory. boris.wiseman@durham.ac.uk

Julian Wright

Julian Wright is a lecturer in History at Durham University and the author of *The Regionalist Movement in France, 1890–1914* (Oxford University Press, 2003). He is currently engaged in a study of the networks, ideas and personal rivalries that underpinned the French socialist movement in the twentieth century. He is deputy editor of the journal *French History*. julian.wright@durham.ac.uk

Paul Yeo

Robert Paul Yeo is a lecturer in Microbiology at Durham University. His research interests focus on RNA viruses, particularly respiratory viruses, and their assembly and replication in cells. His group uses a range of molecular tools to look at the structure of viral components and how they interact to firstly regulate replication and then control how they accumulate in a coordinated manner to form an infectious particle. With colleagues in chemistry Paul's group is applying novel biophysical techniques to the dissection of viral protein interactions with cellular membranes. r.p.yeo@durham.ac.uk

Bennett Zon

Bennett Zon is Professor of Music at Durham University. He studies the role of music in nineteenth- and twentieth-century British culture, with particular interest in the influences of evolutionism and theology. He has published *The English*

Plainchant Revival (Oxford University Press, 1999), *Music and Metaphor in Nineteenth-Century British Musicology* (Ashgate, 2000) and *Representing Non-Western Music in Nineteenth-Century Britain* (University of Rochester Press, 2007). He is general editor of *Nineteenth-Century Music Review* (Ashgate) and the *Music in Nineteenth-Century Britain* book series (Ashgate). bennett.zon@durham.ac.uk

Andrew Heptinstall

Andrew Heptinstall first discovered photography in the late 1970s when in his early teens. A long and varied career path was born from a Russian-built Zenith SLR and a makeshift dark-room in the family bathroom. Andrew has worked in the commercial and advertising sector for over twenty years, after studying photography at Cleveland College of Art & Design, where he was inspired by documentarists such as Don McCullin, Chris Killip and Henri Cartier-Bresson. When Andrew creates images he attempts to capture unique perspectives and encourages the viewer to relive his own experience of that moment in time. With this commission he has relished the chance to return to his roots and rediscover a passion to document the world around him.

Index

drug-addiction 56
Durham Cathedral 219
Durham University 8, 70, 71,
    125, 161, 220
  Department of Computer
    Science 146
  Department of
    Mathematical Sciences
    50
  Department of Physics
    and Psychology 146
  geography department 92
Durkheim, Émile 55
Dworkin, Andrea 186

e-mail 206
Earth
  changing environment 59
  DNA of 11, 68–9
earth sciences 68
earthquakes 68
Easter Island, deforestation
  32
Eastern Eurasia 203
economic behaviour 16
economic development 38
'economic renting' 212
economic theory 187, 188
economists 187
Einstein, Albert 71, 77, 80,
  135
electromagnetic force 80, 81
electromagnetic radiation
  142
electromagnetism 73

electronic publication 204
elegy 11, 13, 26–7
elemental compositions 68
elementary particles 73, 74
Eliot, George 171
  Middlemarch 170
Eliot, T. S.: *The Use of Poetry
  and the Use of Criticism* 167
embryos
  'cloned' 124
  'spare' 124
emotional memory 188
emotion(s)
  driving reason 8, 10–11
  as essential aspects of
    cognition 168
  'standard' emotions 165
'empty space' 70–71
energy consumption 203
enjoyment of life 14
environment, and health
  119–20
environmental archaeology
  111
environmental change 38,
  59
environmental degradation
  111
environmental pollution 119
Ephesus, Turkey 34
equality of the sexes 179
Eritrea 104
Ethiopia 104
  famine 94
ethnic pluralism 45